THE UNITED NATIONS AND A NEW WORLD ORDER FOR A NEW MILLENNIUM

NIJHOFF LAW SPECIALS

VOLUME 44

The United Nations and a New World Order for a New Millennium

Self-determination, State Succession, and Humanitarian Intervention

by:

Edward McWhinney,
Q.C., LL.M., S.J.D., LL.D., M.P.

Barrister and Solicitor,
Professor (Em.) of International Law,
Président de l'Institut de Droit International

KLUWER LAW INTERNATIONAL
THE HAGUE / BOSTON / LONDON

A C.I.P. Catalogue record for this book is available from the Library of Congress.

ISBN 90-411-1371-1

Published by Kluwer Law International,
P.O. Box 85889, 2508 CN The Hague, The Netherlands.

Sold and distributed in North, Central and South America
by Kluwer Law International,
675 Massachusetts Avenue, Cambridge, MA 02139, U.S.A.

In all other countries, sold and distributed
by Kluwer Law International,
P.O. Box 85889, 2508 CN The Hague, The Netherlands.

Printed on acid-free paper

Printed in the Netherlands.

To the memory of
Harold Dwight Lasswell (1902-1978), and
Myres Smith McDougal (1906-1998)

teachers, colleagues, friends.

TABLE OF CONTENTS

ACKNOWLEDGMENTS

Opinions expressed in the present work are those of the author personally and do not engage any of the public and quasi-public institutions or organisations with which the author has been associated over the past decade. No public funds or resources have been expended in the research and preparation of the work. Anna Trinh, B. Comm., has typed all of the manuscript and organised it for publication.

E. McW.

FOREWORD

Failed federal solution for a "difficult" society

The errors – military, political, and not least diplomatic – in the continuing unfolding of the Yugoslav tragedy over the decade since the Fall of the Berlin Wall and the final ending of the Cold War, have a special meaning for those who may have known Yugoslavia in its early configuration, from the 1919 Kingdom of the Serbs, Croats, and the Slovenes on through Tito's Socialist Federal Republic in its successive constitutional formulations. There is a special sadness in contemporary events in the recollection that at certain levels and in very many fields of intellectual action and cooperation, the old Yugoslavia really did function as a multi-ethnic, plural-constitutional society. For some serious students of the federal form, it was even taken as a paradigm or model for building a viable and vibrant plural-constitutional system for a "difficult" society. The contrast was obvious to those federal exercises in what Max Weber had called logico-formal-rationality, – the rather abstract, legalistic federal systems of the blander, ethnically far more homogeneous British Empire and British Commonwealth societies which provided the usual stuff for study by comparative constitutionalists.

I had the pleasure and privilege, in years past when Yugoslavia was still one, to give lectures and have public dialogue in Zagreb and in Belgrade with distinguished scholars like Juraj Andrassy and Milan Bartos and Milos Radojkovic, in the full comprehension that though they were from different communities within Yugoslavia they had a common, optimistic vision of the World Community and its unfolding in the progressive development of International Law under the United Nations Charter. The then Yugoslav jurists were all, of course, united in their opposition to Stalinism and the continuance of the Cold War and of the bipolar division of the World into the two great political-military blocs of the era. We had worked together in international-scientific arenas like the *Institut de Droit International* and the International Law Association in promoting the burgeoning East-West *Détente* and in developing the theoretical legal base in

Peaceful Coexistence/Friendly Relations on which it had to be posited.

With the disintegration of the Socialist Federal Republic of Yugoslavia from the opening of the 1990's onwards, and the rapid descent into regionally-based ethnic conflicts and forms of "ethnic cleansing"practised, as the empirical record has made clear, by all parties and not just one alone, supervening public duties have constrained earlier opportunities the present author had taken to write on new political and political-military problems in the Balkans today and the extent to which they were rooted in past historical conflicts in the region. The author has been able, however, to look at some of the international legal issues concerning the United Nations and the main Western and Western European states that are now directly involved in the continuing Yugoslav crisis, in scientific addresses and lectures and conferences given, variously, to the Aristotle University in Thessaloniki[1] and to the National (Chengchi) University in Taipei[2]; as keynote speaker at the Annual Meeting of the American Branch of the International Law Association[3]; and in several formal depositions before the Committee on Foreign Affairs of the House of Representatives, U.S. Congress, in 1992[4] and 1993[5]. The present work tries to synthesise main ideas advanced in these different legal fora, and also draws on occasional published essays, as in the recently published Festschrift volumes in tribute to Judge (and sometime President) Mohammed Bedjaoui of the International Court of Justice[6] and to the late Judge Li Haopei of the same court[7].

E. McW.
Ottawa and Vancouver

Chapter I

END OF THE MILLENNIUM:
AN ERA OF HISTORICAL TRANSITION

The twentieth century ends, as it had begun, with internecine conflicts in the Balkans. Notwithstanding Bismarck's ironic warning that the Balkans were not worth the bones of a single Pomeranian grenadier, political leaders of the Western World have let themselves be drawn again into complex regional disputes which they have never seemed fully to comprehend or to take the time to study in depth. It all commenced, again, shortly after the fall of the Berlin Wall, with a "premature" recognition, by the German Government, of the sovereignty and independence of several of the constituent republics of the then Socialist Federal Republic of Yugoslavia. This event precipitated the break-down of the complicated set of internal constitutional checks-and-balances that had been carefully put together by Marshal Tito and thereby triggered the dissolution of the Yugoslav entity created by the victors at Versailles in 1919. Western European foreign ministries seemed, at the time, to be reviving, anachronistically, their diplomatic files from the pre-1914 period when the ultimate rival antagonists in World War I had lined up on opposing sides in the settlement of the two Balkan wars of 1912-13.

We live today in an era of historical transition – one of those great periods of very rapid change in society and, of necessity also, in the institutions and processes by which it is governed. Diplomatic history, reflecting the World power base of its time, has been written largely by Western Europeans for the dominant political élites on the World stage, and it has tended to be predominantly Eurocentrist in its content and formulation. Thus the "modern" period in International Relations is held to have begun with the ending of the Thirty Years War in Europe in the mid-17th century and the Treaty of Westphalia of 1648 with its consecration of the prime new international institution and player, the national state. This was in replacement of the old Medieval European concept of public order that was rooted in the institutional dyarchy of the Holy Roman Empire and Holy Roman Church.

It is not always apparent to those who live in a period of revolutionary change that the basic premises of the existing public order system are being challenged and re-defined operationally. Nor are the main trends and directions of the change that is in fact occurring clearly established at the particular moment in time. Those French citizens who stormed the Bastille in 1789 and liberated its few still remaining civil law prisoners, and even the bourgeois intellectuals who engaged in the endless, polite coffee house debates in 1790-1 before the régime of revolutionary Terror had emerged, were hardly aware that they were indeed overthrowing the *ancien régime* and its accumulated body of historical privileges and immunities. The main burthen of Soviet academicians' criticisms of Boris Pasternak's Nobel prize-winning novel, Dr. Zhivago, was that the author rendered as mundane events of love and life in the Russia of 1917 what an expatriate U.S. writer of that earlier time had hailed euphorically, as "Ten days that shook the World". It is left to later generations of authoritative interpreters who write up the sequence of rapidly occurring events, to establish their own preferred historical version as the romantic folklore. Shakespeare's latter-day Tudor-oriented rendition of the monarchical succession in late 15th Century England was to become the accepted historical orthodoxy and judgment on Richard III and the final outcome of the century-long English War of the Roses.

Chapter II

THE PARADIGM SHIFT IN INTERNATIONAL LAW AND RELATIONS

The concept of change – of its necessity and inevitability in the World Community in which we all live today – has been defined and codified by the historian of science, Thomas Kuhn, in his celebrated formulation of the *paradigm shift*.[1] There are elements in his formulation of the thinking of the late 19th century U.S. philosophers, William James and John Dewey, that truth – scientific truth – is not an abstract quality inherent in an idea but something that happens to it: that it is validated operationally by the passage of historical events. On the Kuhn thesis, revolutionary change in scientific thinking, in the Natural Sciences, but of necessity also in the Social Sciences, occurs less by linear projection or incremental extension from existing basic premises, than by sharp, radical breaks with past conventional thinking and the venturing on to new, as yet uncharted frontiers of knowledge. The unbridgeable gap between the Copernican and pre-Copernican visions of the solar system and the rôle of the Earth in relation to the Sun and to the other planets is simply an earlier, at the time theologically shocking, demonstration of an intellectual-scientific paradigm shift with dramatic consequences for all subsequent thinking and research in the discipline concerned.

Public lawyers will find analogues between Kuhn's theory and the development by the great early 20th century Austrian legal theorist, Hans Kelsen, of his Pure Theory of Law.[2] The core concept or intellectual-legal starting point of Kelsen's system was always a *pre*-legal or *meta*-legal sociological or social-political fact – the Basic Premise or *Grundnorm* – from which all supporting legal norms and legal relationships in a society were to be derived, and to which they would always be related back. For Kelsen, the Pure system of law involved a set of logical relationships. The Pure system itself would, by definition, be politically neutral in its dynamic unfolding and law-making, once the initial act – the *extra*-legal, political choice of the authoritative starting point of the whole system – the *Grundnorm* – should have been accepted or imposed.

In examining, in historical retrospect, the past half century in interna-

3

tional relations since the close of hostilities in World War II, it is clear that a number of paradigm shifts have occurred, involving the emergence, *de jure* or *de facto*, of distinct and different *Grundnorms* for World public order, more often operating in succession to each other but sometimes contemporaneously as competing or rival constructs.

(a) The short-lived "One World" paradigm

The One World concept was launched by Wendell Willkie, an unsuccessful Republican candidate for the U.S. Presidency in 1940 when President Roosevelt ran for his third term, and later embraced by leaders of the liberal wing of the Democratic Party, including, after the death of her husband, Mrs. Eleanor Roosevelt who served as a U.S. Ambassador to the United Nations under President Truman. At War's end in 1945, the theme, One World if not the substantive institutions and processes that must go with it, was publicly embraced in the euphoria of the recently victorious Wartime Alliance against Fascism. It was reflected in the new United Nations organisation whose Victors' Consensus was expressed, concretely in constitutional terms, in the dominant Security Council with its five Permanent Members (reflecting a 1945, idealised version of global political-military power after Germany and Japan's defeat), and with those Permanent Members having a legal right of veto over all substantive decisions to be reached by the new World organisation. It is perhaps also to be seen in the unfortunately short-lived Baruch Plan of 1946 for a sharing of the new Atomic Energy.

The One World premise, with its *Grundnorm* rooted in the notion of a World government located in the United Nations itself, was soon rudely shattered by the rapid onset of the Cold War and the emergence of a *de facto* Bipolar system of World public order resting on confrontation and then accommodation of the twin, political-military Blocs, Soviet and Western, controlled effectively by the Bloc leaders, the Soviet Union and the United States, and dominating between them the whole of the World Community.

(b) The Cold War Bipolar paradigm

One of the immediate consequences of the new Bipolarity was the jelling of the territorial status quo that had been sanctioned politically at the

4

Roosevelt–Churchill–Stalin summit meeting at Yalta in early 1945, and then legally confirmed, on a putatively temporary basis, at War's end in Europe and East Asia in 1945, in the Military surrender and truce agreements. Bipolarity meant a perpetuation of the politically divided states, – Germany and Korea, as the prime examples, – that had been envisaged and sanctioned at the wartime summit meetings of the heads of the anti-Axis alliance and then concretised in political-military terms in the late 1945 military cease-fires and military capitulations in Europe and in Asia. But, except for the very early years when the East-West ideological conflict and the ensuing rhetorical battles in the United Nations were at their height, the Cold War emerges, in historical retrospect, as very much more ordered and predictable, and also rational in historical terms, in its respect for elementary power considerations and conventional balance-of-power arguments, than was always understood or appreciated when the Cold War was at its rhetorical and propaganda height. For the more than four decades of the Cold War's duration, from War's end in 1945 to the symbolic falling of the Berlin Wall in 1989, the political-military lines of territorial demarcation were in fact fairly generally respected and maintained, on both sides, Soviet and Western alike.

There were, to be sure, continuing probings or testings for points of weakness or ambiguity in peripheral areas where the respective Blocs' interests had not always been clearly defined or maintained, as in Korea in the summer of 1950 (where an earlier address by U.S. Secretary of State, Dean Acheson, had seemed to indicate Korea was not within the U.S.-defined sphere of influence); or in Berlin, with the Soviet blockade of land access in the late 1940s, something not envisaged and in consequence not very clearly defined in the Yalta and Potsdam allied settlements of 1945; or even in Cuba, in 1962, when Khrushchev ventured, in a rashly daring gambler's gesture, to introduce Soviet intermediate-range missiles within a region always considered by the United States, since the early 19th century Monroe Doctrine and certainly since the Spanish-American War of 1898, to be a U.S. sphere of influence. Once the Cuban Missile crisis had been successfully resolved, however, through direct personal summit diplomacy by the two Bloc leaders, Khrushchev and Kennedy, at the end of October, 1962, the Cold War *de facto* system of World public order, and its territorial divisions and allocations, and its political-military spheres of influence, were not again to be seriously challenged or questioned.

(c) The Peaceful Coexistence/Friendly Relations continuum

What emerged, in fact, was a consolidation and legitimation of the political-military status quo of 1945, – a sort of Metternichean settlement on a *Pax Sovietica-Americana* basis. The operational methodology and process for negotiation and international law-making during the Cold War in its post-Stalin, what-might-be-called "mature", period flowed logically and inevitably from its Bipolar paradigm or model of World public order: direct, bilateral diplomacy between the two Bloc leaders, preferably in Summit Meetings *à deux*, followed by model treaties reflecting the Bloc leaders' own Bipolar consensus and then presented, after their own bilateral negotiation and drafting, to the lesser, supporting Bloc members on either side for signature and ratification, and this normally without the possibility of serious modification or amendment on their part. In terms of concrete problem-solving, the two rival Bloc leaders, the Soviet Union and the United States, increasingly put behind them the coloured language and ideological rhetoric of the very early, Stalinist, Cold War years. The change had come with the transition from Stalin to Khrushchev and the inauguration, in 1956, of the official de-Stalinisation campaign within the Soviet Union. The legal spokesman on the Soviet side was the then legal Adviser to the Soviet Foreign Ministry, Gregory Tunkin, who was also a personal adviser to Khrushchev on foreign policy issues. Tunkin was the principal author of the Soviet doctrinal campaign, launched in the United Nations and numbers of other major international legal arenas, in behalf of Peaceful Coexistence. The doctrine was formulated at a very high level of abstraction and in *a priori* terms only. It was sought to be linked historically, by its Soviet authors, to the Panch Shila Agreement of 1954 between the People's Republic of China and India. Khrushchev, in his address to the 22nd Congress of the Communist Party in 1961, attributed the original source to Lenin and as having "always been the central feature of Soviet foreign policy". Its primary principles were listed in Professor Kozhevnikov's official Soviet textbook of the time on International Law, as follows:

mutual respect for territorial integrity and sovereignty; non-aggression; non-interference in internal affairs; equality and mutual advantage.[3]

In historical retrospect, these postulated primary principles of Peaceful Coexistence seem harmless enough and to be found, anyway, in the mainsprings of classical Western conceptions of International Law. Peaceful Coexistence was, however, viewed initially by Western foreign ministries with deep reserve and suspicion, as a Trojan Horse device to allow the Soviet Union to talk of peace and lull the West into a false sense of security while Soviet rearmament and military expansionist drives continued apace. The desire in Western foreign ministries to develop a sophisticated Western doctrinal-legal response and defence against the Soviet doctrinal-legal campaign led to the debate being transferred from official inter-governmental legal arenas to private, scientific and academic-legal fora. There was a veritable "battle of the books" conducted in the Soviet Yearbook of International Law and the journal, Soviet State and Law, and replicated in the main French and U.S. Law journals, and continued in a number of specialist monographs on each side. But the main such forum, in the early formative years of the Coexistence debate, became the London-based International Law Association, a private organisation of practising lawyers and government and international functionaries in which, by happy accident, Soviet jurists and Soviet bloc jurists of the intellectual calibre of Gregory Tunkin and Manfred Lachs (later Polish judge on the World Court and then the Court President) had participated over a number of years. Balancing the Soviet bloc representation were Western jurists like John Hazard, the leading U.S. scholar on Soviet law, and Maître Henri Cochaux of the Brussells Bar, and Non-Aligned countries' representatives such as Krishna Rao, Legal Adviser to the Indian Foreign Ministry, and Milan Bartos and Milos Radojkovic from Yugoslavia. The extensive East-West debates and exchanges on Peaceful Co-existence at the biennial reunions of the International Law Association, beginning in 1956, and continuing through the 1960's, spawned a later, parallel action in the main official, inter-governmental arena, the United Nations General Assembly. Under the somewhat inelegant but politically colourless euphemism, Friendly Relations and Cooperation among States (this in replacement for the term, Peaceful Coexistence, which had become anathema to some Western foreign ministries), a 27-country (later 31-country) Special Committee was established by U.N. General Assembly Resolution 1966 (XVIII) of 16 December 1963, and charged with the "progressive development and codification" of what were, essentially, the five International Law principles specified in the original Soviet list of principles of Coexistence. Seven years later, the Special Committee had completed its work with a Declaration on Principles of International Law concerning Friendly Relations and Cooperation among States in accordance with the Charter of the United Nations, which was formally embodied in the U.N. General Assembly Resolution 2625 (XXV) of 24 October 1970.

By the time of the legal enactment in 1970, the establishment of principles of Friendly Relations had come as something of a political anti-climax. The main dialectical-legal battle between Soviet and Soviet bloc jurists who had campaigned, originally, for a single act of codification and listing of a set of abstract, *a priori*, so-called "primary" principles, and Western and non-aligned jurists who had argued, instead, for rendering the concept precise and operational in terms of concrete secondary principles which would be derived inductively from actual East-West legal problem-situations and their solutions, had been resolved practically, by achieving both objectives at the same time. The Soviet jurists had their Code, now sanctified at long last in the U.N. General Assembly's Resolution on Friendly Relations of 1970. At the same time, the Western jurists' emphasis on concrete solution of actual East-West tension-issues had been vindicated in what might be called an operational code or methodology for East-West conflicts-resolution. This was the pragmatic, empirical, problem-oriented, step-by-step approach, which gave priority to inter-Bloc problem-solving and to the solution of long-standing or immediate collisions of vital interests on a basis of mutuality and reciprocity of interest as between the two rival political-military blocs, Soviet and Western, and also their leaders. This became the operational methodology of *Détente*, leading on to the creation of a substantive body of International Law of *Détente*[4], derived from the interaction of the two rival blocs and their pragmatic accommodation on a case-by-case basis. It was most strikingly demonstrated in the series of East-West nuclear and general disarmament treaties, throughout the *Détente* period of the 1960s and 1970s.[5] It was also vindicated with the special European security treaties of the early 1970s, both the series of special bilateral treaties between the then West Germany and all of its Eastern neighbours over legitimation of existing *de facto* territorial frontiers in Middle and Eastern Europe (the Ostpolitik treaties), but also the comprehensive, overarching pan-European security treaty, the Helsinki Final Act of 1975.

The key point in these elaborate exercises, apart from their refreshing emphasis on dialogue rather than direct military action, is that they served to recognise and ultimately to legitimate the political-military *status quo* that had been licensed by the Yalta Accord of early 1945 and the subsequent military capitulation arrangements at War's end. They accepted the balance of power, the classical political principle controlling and regulating international relations throughout its "modern" period from the Treaty of Westphalia on to the present.

The distinguished historian of international relations, Samuel Huntingon, has advanced the rather novel and intellectually provoking thesis that Western liberal-democratic leaders and diplomats were able to carry on serious negotiation and fruitful intellectual dialogue with Soviet Marxist-trained leaders and diplomats, during this prolonged Cold War period, because both Liberalism and Marxism had common Western sources.[6] A *Realpolitik*-oriented interpretation might, however, also direct attention to the increasingly static, conservative nature of their own long-range interests as identified by both superpowers. The United States and the Soviet Union, as the Cold War matured into *Détente*, were experiencing difficulties, in common, in reaching political accommodation with the new majorities in the United Nations and in the U.N. General Assembly in particular that had been created by the admission as new member-states of the organisation, from the end of the 1950s and throughout the 1960s, of a flood of new, Third World countries established in the wake of Decolonisation, Independence, and Self-determination on a World-wide scale. The Winds of Change in the World Community unleashed by the delayed collapse of the pre-War European colonial empires, created vast new tensions and new demands which could only with great difficulty be accommodated or satisfied within the, by now, increasingly outmoded Bipolar World public order system. The bureaucratic inertia and repressiveness of the Soviet system, and a certain lack of imagination or new thinking on entirely new problems on the part of the United States – in Vietnam and in Nicaragua, as merely the more notable examples – were all reflections of an international society in rapid historical transition in response to new societal forces, and of the inability or unwillingness of the then governing political élites to make changes while they were still timely and before the situation should have become pathological and politically out-of-hand. This fundamental contradiction or antinomy, by the 1980s, between what was, by that time, an already out-of-date World public order system and the emerging new set of political and social forces in the World Community, was perhaps temporarily veiled by the fall of the Berlin Wall in 1989 and the resulting sudden collapse of the Soviet Union and the ending of the Cold War. (It was then Soviet President Gorbachev who made the historically timely and courageously far-sighted decision not to call on Soviet military force to control mounting popular unrest and dissension in East Germany, unlike his predecessor, Brezhnev, in Czechoslovakia in 1968). There were those, then, like Francis Fukuyama, who reacted no doubt too quickly, in the euphoria of the rapidly unfolding events, by postulating as the historical outcome the triumph on a global scale of Western liberal-democracy and, in consequence, an "end of history" in its special, post-Renaissance, Western European vision as a dialectical process of

9

ascertainment and development of truth through the competition and inter-action of opposing schools of thought.[7]

(d) An operational code for inter-bloc relations in the era of *Détente*: the East-West "rules of the game"

The East-West "great debate" over Coexistence/Friendly Relations lasted a full decade and a half, from the late 1950s to the opening of the 1970s. In highly pragmatic fashion, it reconciled and synthesised two rather different methodological approaches to East-West conflicts-resolution whose differences seemed to stem as much from the dichotomy of basic Common Law/Civil Law modes of legal reasoning as from issues of ultimate ideological choice. On the Soviet side, the programme outlined by Secretary Khrushchev and his supporting jurists had called for a single great act of codification of postulated abstract, *a priori* legal principles. On the Western side, there was an evident horror in debating philosophic absolutes and an emphasis instead on fairly low-level problem-solving and on dealing quickly and concretely with actual tension-issues in inter-bloc relations as they should arise from time to time. On the one side, as the negotiation starting point, the Sermon on the Mount! On the other side a "politic of little steps" and case-by-case development of inter-bloc accommodations, without any conscious search for over-riding general principles. In fact, as the East-West dialogue was entered upon, both protagonists achieved what they had asked for. The two different approaches occurred by separate, parallel routes and reached successful conclusion about the same time, by the opening of the 1970s: on the one hand the United Nations General Assembly's celebrated Declaration of Principles on Friendly Relations and Cooperation among States, of October, 1970, and on the other a whole series of East-West bilateral accords (often translated into larger, near universal multilateral accords) advanced by essentially pragmatic, empirical diplomatic negotiating teams on a problem-oriented, step-by-step basis.

As key demonstration of this latter, problem-oriented approach, we have the series of treaties devoted respectively to the guarantee of the legitimacy and security of the territorial frontiers and dispositions arising from the recent War, and to nuclear and general disarmament. As the major affirmation of the other, more strictly "principled" approach, we have the 1970 General Assembly Declaration's restatement in a special, Cold War context, of the United Nations Charter's stipulations on the illegality of the

10

use of armed force as a solvent for international differences, and on the maintenance of international peace and security.

To this catalogue of legal rights-duties relationships we may add more informal, but no less well respected developed practice or custom as between the two blocs – what might be called Cold War ground rules or "rules-of-the-game". These ground rules cover a wide spectrum of inter-bloc practice, deriving usually from considerations of mutual advantage and reciprocal give-and-take. Among these are, certainly, the rules of avoidance of surprise in inter-bloc and international relations generally, lest the sudden and unexpected should provoke an overly-hasty and irrational response on the other side. What was in origin simple custom resting on ordinary common-sense, became concretised, not too long after the Cuban Missile crisis of 1962 with its obvious lessons on the dangers of unilateral actions which might catch the other side unaware, by the creation in the mid 1960s of the Hot-line direct communication system between the two bloc leaders. In other aspects, however, the Coexistence/Friendly Relations debate, as it unfolded, revealed the politically conservative, even reactionary, Metternichean aspect of emerging *Détente*. Herein was the legitimation of that territorial *status quo* sanctioned by the great political-military settlements arrived at by the Allied leaders, – the Big Three and later Big Five, – at their conclaves in Yalta and Potsdam and elsewhere, which effectively divided Europe in two; and which also consecrated "spheres of influence" attributed to either bloc leader in buffer state zones being between their respective regions or in newly divided states (the two Germanies and the two Koreas, as the prime examples), or in other areas which, because of lack of time or simple oversight, had failed to be fully identified or assigned by the Allied leaders in their wartime conferences. The Soviet Union's hegemonial interventions in Hungary in 1956 and in Czechoslovakia in 1968, silently acquiesced in or tolerated by the other bloc at the time, and the U.S. assertion of a form of latter-day Monroe Doctrine in the Bay of Pigs sortie into Cuba in 1961, with related incursions in Guatemala, Nicaragua and Panama at various times throughout the Cold War, all fall into this category. Throughout this time, however, the dialectical processes of progressive development of International Law, in accordance with the United Nations Charter, can be observed in full operation. In a dynamic unfolding of new ground rules and new principles, what started off as a form of strictly limited, armed truce between two irreconcilable ideological antagonists shaded off, more and more, into elementary rules of common-sense and mutual respect and tolerance.

11

It became a vindication of President De Gaulle's maxim uttered at the end of the 1960s, with its built-in prophesy for the future: *Détente, Entente, Coopération.*

Chapter III

THE POST-COLD WAR ERA:
THE END OF THE "END OF HISTORY"

Another paradigm shift with, this time, a *Pax Americana* presided over and, if need be, militarily and unilateral-militarily enforced by the United States on the pattern of the celebrated 19th century *Pax Britannica* that had been financially underwritten by the Pound Sterling and unilaterally imposed by the British Navy, would be an obvious, logical conclusion from Fukuyama's reasoning, as the new basic premise of a resulting new World public order system. And yet such a *Pax Americana* has not so far acquired general recognition or acceptance as the paradigm or model for the post-Cold War World Community. With the disappearance of the Bipolar system of World order following the end of the Cold War and the collapse of the Soviet Empire, at least two competing models have emerged. The one is Unipolar and projected from the United States. The other is much more diffused or plural and based upon the United Nations as a Polypolar system of World order in which a number of different powers or groupings of powers would compete or coexist with each other, without any one being predominant in relation to the others. The latter paradigm shift had appeared more probable in the early 1990's because of the relative decline, then, with the ending of the Cold War, of the military-logistical (and especially nuclear-military) underpinnings of the World Public Order system and also the entry of new financial and commercial determinants in which non-nuclear powers like Japan and the new Asian economic "Tigers" would be able (in spite of some, no doubt temporary set-backs such as were to occur in 1998), to compete with or challenge the erstwhile hegemony of older, more traditional World powers.

The practical consequences, in International law terms, of the antinomy between two such radically different contemporary paradigms of World order – the Unipolar and the Polypolar – were demonstrated in the December, 1998, renewal of the military operations in the Persian Gulf. In the earliest, 1990-1 Gulf War, President Bush had been able to rally a substantial number of allies, up to thirty states, including the main Arab, Islamic states of the Middle East region, in varying degrees of political-military logistical involvement in support of the collective security measures against Iraq that had been spearheaded by the United States' own massive, direct military operations in the desert. This had all been done under the express authority of United Nations Security Council Resolutions and carried out under U.S. military command, with the stated design to restore and maintain the territorial integrity of Kuwait and its original frontiers, after the invasion by Iraq.

But, seven years later, only the United States and the former Middle East regional, Colonial, Mandatory power, Great Britain, were prepared to venture on fresh direct military action in Iraq at the U.S. President's call. The U.S. and Great Britain fell back, as legal justification for their new military action in the Gulf region against Iraq, on the earlier Security Council Resolutions from the Gulf War period. But these Security Council Resolutions had all been enacted in another time and, arguably, enacted for another, different political situation and for a different political purpose.

Contemporary legal doctrines had elevated to the rank of Jus Cogens, as a constitutional-legal absolute under the United Nations Charter and an imperative principle of the new International Law, the Charter prohibition on the Use of Force as a means of resolving international disputes, with the only exception to this being the right of self-defence conceded under Article 51 of the Charter. Such an absolute prohibition of the Use of Force could only be legally dispensed with, on this view, by a specific U.N. Security Council Resolution, expressly adopted under Chapter VII of the U.N. Charter for that purpose, in a particular, precisely-defined problem-situation. This had been the position maintained by the current U.N. Secretary-General and, consistently, by his predecessors, and it was evidently supported by those states that chose not to respond to the diplomatic pressures exercised upon them by the U.S. and Great Britain to take part directly in the December, 1998, renewed military operations in the Gulf region.

In a situation of competing paradigms of World order, with the substantially different legal consequences deriving logically, in Kelsenian terms, from each one of them, it is, arguably, unacceptable that any one state or group of states should be able to claim the right to decide, and then to act unilaterally, on recourse to armed force (this, in the absence of a *bona fide* situation of self-defense, as defined in the United Nations Charter). For that would be a situation of one party, only, to an international dispute acting, in effect, as judge, jury, and executioner in its own behalf. An obvious remedy in any such situation, would be recourse to authoritative Third Party settlement, judicial or arbitral. The International Court of Justice, in its *Lockerbie* ruling[1], manifested a new tendency to pick up the torch from the very effective national constitutional courts of post-War Europe; and, also, in supplement to its more traditional *inter partes* jurisdiction, to essay new definitions of constitutional power and its constitutional-legal limits within the United Nations, and to rule on the proper allocation and distribution of law-making competence as between the different United Nations organs – General Assembly, Security Council, the office of the Secretary-General, and the Court itself.

In the Kosovo situation of March, 1999, a latter-day, residual problem surviving from the various Western European powers' non-action or failures in peaceful regulation of the State Succession to Tito's Socialist Federal Republic of Yugoslavia, the United States and its Western European associates chose to overlook or simply forgot the pragmatic reconciliation of the sometimes competing Law and Power imperatives that had been achieved by President Kennedy and Secretary Khrushchev in the Cuban Missile crisis of October, 1962. The two Bloc leaders, in that situation, opted finally for the alternative, more moderate, *legal* controls not involving recourse to armed force. The Kennedy-Khrushchev peaceful resolution, through diplomatic means in 1962, of a crisis that took the World Community to the brink of nuclear war is rightly celebrated today as a textbook example of international problem-solving in tension-situations. In contrast, in the Kosovo situation, the principal Western political players may have broken off the Rambouillet diplomatic negotiation processes prematurely in favour of direct military action. The chosen instrument for recourse to armed force in that case was the vestigial, Cold War era, Western military alliance, NATO. There was no approach by the member-states of the NATO military group to the United Nations Security Council for a legal dispensation from the U.N. Charter's legal interdiction of the Use of Force – the condition precedent to international peace-*making* action under Chapter VII of the Charter. The publicly advanced argument of the NATO states' Foreign Ministers for avoiding the United Nations in this way was the expressed fear that a legal Veto would be applied in the Security Council by either one of the two *non*-NATO Permanent Members of the Security Council, Russia and China. But the fact remains that the hypothesis of a Permanent Member Veto was never actually tried and tested by the NATO member-states in the most obvious and most direct way of actually submitting a draft Resolution for consideration and debate in the Security Council. More surprising, however, was the failure of NATO member-states, and especially the United States, to proceed in the alternative United Nations law-making arena, the U.N. General Assembly, on the precedent of the Uniting-for-Peace Resolution that had been successfully

15

sponsored by President Truman and then Secretary of State Dean Acheson in the Korean War crisis of 1950, in anticipation at that time of just such a Permanent Member's legal Veto being applied in the Security Council. The celebrated Resolution 377A(V) had been adopted by the U.N. General Assembly on 3 November 1950, on the initiative of the United States, by vote of 52 to 5 with 2 abstentions. The General Assembly Resolution proclaimed the full legal authority of the General Assembly to legislate to fill the gap as to international peace-making – "if the Security Council, because of lack of unanimity of the permanent members, fails to exercise its primary responsibility for the maintenance of international peace and security in any case". The Uniting-for-Peace process, exercised through the U.N. General Assembly, remains to this day as an authoritative constitutional-legal precedent for United Nations action, in default of Security Council initiatives that may have failed because of application in the Security Council of a Permanent Member's Veto. In the General Assembly there is, of course, no Permanent Member's Veto, a simple two-thirds majority being legally sufficient to enact any deemed "important" (non-procedural) measure. It has been speculated that the U.S Administration's eschewing of the U.N. Security Council processes as to international peace-making without any prior attempt at actually testing the Security Council's will on Kosovo, and then the avoidance by the U.S. State Department of its own Uniting-for-Peace precedent from 1950 through the alternative, General Assembly route, reflected a long-standing U.S. visceral distrust or dislike of the United Nations as a whole. This U.S. attitude had been evidenced earlier in the (successful) U.S. campaign within the United Nations in 1995 to bar an activist, reform-minded, incumbent U.N. Secretary-General, Boutros Boutros-Ghali, from a second term (2); and it had been evidenced also in the sustained U.S. refusal, over the years, to pay the full amount of the U.S.-assessed contributions to the U.N.'s annual budgets. In the result, however, without a prior legal authorisation from the United Nations, whether from the Security Council or from the General Assembly, the NATO direct military action against Yugoslavia was left without any apparent, affirmative legal base and justification in International Law. The chosen instrument for the direct military action against Yugoslavia – NATO – as a subordinate, regional, collective security organisation, would remain at all times legally subject to and controlled by the express stipulations in the U.N. Charter outlawing the Use of Force. NATO could not hoist itself by its own bootstraps into a legal power not expressly and in terms given to it by the U.N. Charter nor authorised, as such, by the appropriate principal organs of the United Nations.

Chapter IV

PARADIGM COMPETITION IN AN ERA OF TRANSITION: CHANGING SOCIETAL TRENDS AND CONDITIONS

An era of historical transition, such as the present, is always marked by the competition and interaction of radically different conceptions of its own contemporary international society, and also of the preferred direction in which the World Community should move for the future. Key societal factors which may effectively condition and control national and international policy-making today, are identified hereunder.

(a) Movement from a political-military to a political-economic base of World order

In spite of the Gulf War and of the most recent NATO military action against Yugoslavia which, on some views, takes on elements of earlier historical stereotypes of armed intervention, there has been a perceptible shift in the World Community from a political-military to a political-economic base of World public order, with the ending of the Cold War. This involves not merely the paradox that some states, like the former Soviet Union, that remain superpowers in strictly military terms because of their continuing status as one of the five member-states of the "Nuclear Weapons Club", may, at least for the moment, have sunk to the level of second or third rank states in purely economic terms. It also means that some of the other, economically better-off states that are also members of the Nuclear Weapons Club, like Great Britain and France, may need to re-think and re-order national planning policies that have seen too much of their national treasure and their national intellectual-scientific resources devoted to nuclear and general rearmament and to a strong military posture redolent of bygone 19th century Imperial glory. In retrospect, as one of those unintended historical ironies, it may have been very fortunate for the World War II losers, Germany and Japan, that under the Carthaginian peace settlements imposed on them in the military capitulations of 1945 they were deprived of both the constitutional right and also the political opportunity to enter the nuclear arms race, and forced, in default, to concentrate on financial and economic rebuilding and industrial modernisation. The economic miracle so quickly achieved, post-War, by both Germany and Japan, may have stemmed in measure from their ability to concentrate on pure research in science and technology and engineering, unencumbered by competing demands of national defence priorities.

(b) Accentuated rôle of international finance and trade arenas

The shift from a political-military to a political-economic base of World public order has meant an accentuation of the political importance and the effective decision-making rôle of those international fora and agencies whose special competence and legal jurisdiction and mandate are the negotiation and development of international trade and commerce. The original hope of the United Nations' Founding Fathers in 1945 for a World trade body to accompany the new United Nations organisation, had had to be down-graded to the complicated, informal, ad hoc arrangements and accommodations and processes of the GATT. A high degree of functional efficacy in international trade was achieved, nevertheless, by these substitute means. But it has now all given way to the new World Trade Organization which, with the World Bank and the International Monetary Fund, looks like becoming the prime international arena in the new Millennium, outpacing the U.N. Security Council and General Assembly since taking over the key economic and financial decisions and decision-making issues from those other institutions. It is, in this sense, speculated that the World Trade tribunal in Geneva, by virtue of its specialist jurisdiction and the sort of cases it is called upon to regulate, could even become more important than the International Court of Justice in the range of key political and political-economic issues that it will be called upon to resolve by legal means.

(c) Trans-national economic integration and regional association

Parallel to the shift from the political-*military* to the political-*economic* base of world public order, there is a major trend to trans-national financial and economic association and cooperation on a regional basis, often involving high degrees of supra-national constitutional-legal integration.

18

While the European Union is the best and longest established of the examples, similar developments are to be seen in the Canada-U.S. Free Trade Agreement and in the Canada-U.S.-Mexico (trilateral) free trade agreement, the latter agreement to be extended to include Chile and with further Latin American candidates short-listed. Within Latin America itself, similar regional arrangements are now under way. This new, supra-national integration on a regional basis should, long-range, also strengthen *One World*, United Nations-based constitutional arrangements through its creation of new patterns of regional interdependence across conventional territorial frontiers. But there will be new necessities to try to coordinate and harmonise those special regional arrangements with the U.N. and with U.N.-agencies-based powers and actions. The new regional economic associations have given a certain preemptive leadership to the economically most powerful member-state, the United States, paralleling the effective power and command over lesser, supporting states exercised by the U.S. during the Cold War in relation to the members of the Western political-military bloc. A more pluralistic approach to general foreign policy and policy-making within the regional economic bloc may, however, be one of the first casualties, if the Gulf War and the Kosovo operation are to be taken as an indication.

(d) Historical resurgence of nationalism and ethno-cultural particularism

Coexisting with these new trends to supra-nationalism and co-operation across conventional state frontiers, conventionally defined, has been the resurgence of nationalism and ethno-cultural particularism, in the wake of the ending of the Cold War and the Bipolar world order system. Under the Cold War system of World Public Order, the two Bloc leaders had clearly preferred stability and predictability – the status quo of existing territorial frontiers and of the late 19th century definitions of state sovereignty – over the pressures for change and rectification of past historical errors or injustices stemming, for example, from the two Balkan Wars of 1912-13 and the supporting Central and Eastern European treaties to the larger Versailles Treaty of 1919. It cannot be said that the present-day Concert of Europe – the Western European Foreign Ministers who presided over the effective dissolution and the resulting State Succession to the former Socialist Federal Republic of Yugoslavia – really understood how practically to reconcile the conflicting political interests and demands in South-

Eastern Europe and the Balkans of peace and security on the one hand and the International Law principle of self-determination of peoples on the other. This new Concert of Europe (Western Europe) at the opening of the 1990's singularly lacked the larger vision and imagination displayed by Bismarck and Disraeli at the Congress of Berlin in 1878, more than a century earlier. The European Foreign Ministers at the opening of the 1990s, in default of a larger intellectual vision of the post-Cold War World and of a new, pan-European public order seemed, anachronistically, to be reviving their own national Foreign Ministry legal briefs from the time of the pre-World War I conflicts between the main European powers of that earlier day. The academic experiments in a new form of federalism within Bosnia-Herzegovina intended to fill the power vacuum left by the premature dissolution of Titoist Yugoslavia, that were ventured on in the United Nations sponsored Vance-Owen and then Owen-Stoltenberg plans, whose principal authors had never themselves lived within a genuinely plural-ethnic constitutional system, had from the beginning a curious element of artificiality and political unreality and always seemed threatened with political disaster, long-range. The U.N. Peace-*keeping* and Peace-*making* operations (the political, if not the legal line between Chapter VI and Chapter VII of the U.N. Charter is not always easy to draw), in post-Succession Yugoslavia became, inevitably, stop-gap in the absence of a clear and coherent design for future overall regional development and cooperation.

In their approach to the Kosovo situation in 1999, the political and military leaders of the NATO military alliance seem to have learnt nothing and forgotten nothing from the bitter lessons of the Bosnia-Herzegovina internecine conflicts and of the political fragility of the internal territorial frontiers left behind from Titoist federal Yugoslavia. In particular, the NATO powers seem hardly to have foreseen the "falling dominoes" effect of still further external political tampering with those frontiers, both upon fragile new Succession states like FYROM-Macedonia and also upon longer-standing neighbouring states having their own large ethno-cultural minorities. On many views, the NATO intervention, without the benefit of any prior, overriding, comprehensive political plan, may have exacerbated, rather than diminished, existing ethnic conflicts within the larger Balkan region.

(e) Participatory Democracy and the new, People's power in international relations

A potentially unsettling, though long-range possibly liberating, factor in International law-making in the current era of historical transition, has been the emergence in international policy-making of what has been called, in municipal, national politics, People's Power (Participatory Democracy). The new People's Power takes advantage to the full of the new instruments of direct mass communication, through FAX and Web-site and the current cut-rate charges for international telephone conference calls. The Land Mines Treaty, signed in Ottawa at the beginning of December, 1997, by 120 states and then entering into International Law force a bare ten months later with the deposing of the necessary minimum number of forty instruments of state ratification, is a rather startling example of the success of this new, trans-national, populist approach to international law-making. Across conventional state frontiers, religious and other "peace" groups joined forces with the medical and health groups specially involved in caring for non-combatant, civilian and especially child victims of land mines planted by the rival forces in mostly undeclared Third World civil wars or armed combats. National special interest groups of this sort lobbied their own national foreign ministries for an International Law ban on the production, manufacture, export and sale of these particularly vicious and destructive weapons of modern armed conflicts that have been demonstrated to persist in their effects long after the original conflicts have ceased and the original, regular or irregular armed combatants have gone home. After successfully lobbying their own (mostly Western, middle-rank state) foreign ministries, the non-governmental groups involved in that movement proceeded to network with church, academic, professional, and scientific-medical interest groups in other countries around the World. In fact the fortieth state to ratify the Land Mines Treaty and thus bring it into legal force in 1998 was a Third World state, Burkina Faso, and its adherence to the treaty had been directly promoted by trans-national exchange between non-governmental groups from original Western sponsor states and similar peer groups within Burkina Faso. The signal, rapid success of the trans-national, populist-based Land Mines Treaty process led on to the subsequent, much accelerated achievement, in July 1998, of the signing in Rome of a general Treaty establishing a new International Criminal Court. This was done to an evident political dismay, (and in some cases at least in spite of the negative diplomatic efforts) of some at least of the Permanent Members of the United Nations Security Council. Such determined Big-

Power opposition may be enough in itself to hold up or delay ratification and entry into legal force of the International Criminal Court treaty, for which no less than 60 state ratifications are needed. But it is unlikely to hinder the new People's Power and popular involvement in an international law-making process that is widely perceived as having been, heretofore, an arcane exercise appropriated by political leaders and attendant bureaucratic advisers and not always open, therefore, to the Winds of Change in the contemporary World Community and in an International Law that is supposed to reflect contemporary societal needs and expectations. [2]

(f) State and Governmental responsibility in international criminal law

One no doubt unintended consequence of the NATO-directed armed intervention in Yugoslavia in 1999 has been the suggestion for extension to the main political and military actors on both sides of that conflict of the principle of universality of international criminal law responsibility. This had been argued for by some of the proponents of the new, general jurisdiction, International Criminal Court, and had been resisted in turn by key Permanent Members of the U.N. Security Council. The United Nations Commissioner for Human Rights, former President of Ireland, Mary Robinson, had made the point that the *ad hoc* War Crimes tribunal for Yugoslavia should indeed have authority to investigate the military actions of *all* participants in the Kosovo conflict, including in this the NATO political and military leadership with regard to the civilian deaths and injuries inflicted by the high-level aerial bombardments of Belgrade and other Yugoslav cities. The "smart bombs", aimed with pin-point precision at military targets only, had proved not to be so accurate after all. NATO officials had excused such bombing of civilian populations and civil targets as "collateral" or "incidental" damage only – unfortunate accidents – and had offered public expressions of apologies. However, the contemporary International Law as to aerial bombardment, contained in the Protocols Additional to the Geneva Conventions of 1949 (Protection of Victims of International Armed Conflicts), adopted in 1977, included in the legal proscriptions of indiscriminate attacks those which – "may be expected to cause incidental loss of civilian life, injury to civilians, damage to civilian objects, or a combination thereof, which would be excessive in relation to the concrete and direct military advantage anticipated." (1977 Additional Protocols, Part IV, Civilian Population, Chapter II, Article 51(4)). Beyond that, the NATO aerial bombardment of the Chinese Embassy in Belgrade, with resultant loss of life and injuries to Chinese diplomatic personnel, may also have breached the legal rules on specially protected diplomatic and other personnel, which in Customary International Law and also more recent legal codifications have achieved a *Jus Cogens* quality. An *a priori* U.N. Security Council enabling Resolution of the nature of those adopted for the Gulf War military operation in 1990-1, might have cured the problem. In its absence, an important legal gap appeared to remain as to legal responsibility.

(g) Legality of nuclear weapons

In the early 1990's, disappointed by the evident failure of the acknowledged five existing members of the "Nuclear Weapons Club" (all five of the Permanent Members of the U.N. Security Council), to honour their legal obligation, under the Non-Proliferation Treaty of 1968, to proceed in timely fashion to negotiate the elimination of all their own nuclear weapons and nuclear weapon stockpiles, a "ginger group" of U.S. and European international lawyers in New York and Amsterdam (IALANA), organised a campaign to have the International Court of Justice rule on the legality of nuclear weapons and of their use in armed combat. The specialist group's work involved preparing the technical legal briefs and also providing or funding expert legal counsel and advisers for states otherwise lacking in funds that might be encouraged to raise the issue in the U.N. General Assembly and in the specialised U.N. Agency, the World Health Organisation. What was sought was an Advisory Opinion reference to the World Court that might result in a Court declaration that nuclear weapons are outlawed under contemporary International Law. The political campaign within the United Nations to secure the Advisory Opinion reference to the International Court was eventually successful. Though the actual ruling by the Court disappointed some with its multiplicity of Separate Opinions by individual judges and also with the absence of a clear, affirmative ruling by the Court on the main substantive issue of illegality of nuclear weapons, the Court did indeed hold that there is a present legal obligation of states that now have nuclear weapons to proceed to negotiate their abolition. Failure by the five "Nuclear Weapons Club" members to proceed on this obligation "with all deliberate speed", might carry the risk of rendering as legally licit action by non-Nuclear Weapons Club members to move in their own conceived self-interest and self-defence and to endow themselves with their own nuclear weapons. In this regard, the mid-1998 nuclear test explosions by India and then by Pakistan were evidently designed with a view to larger, Asian, regional security considerations, the People's Republic of China being a member of the "Nuclear Weapons Club". In the aftermath of the NATO military action against Yugoslavia, possession of one's own nuclear weapons and long-range delivery systems, might appear to some states as a necessary political-military investment: on the experience of the Cold War, it could, arguably, provide balance and deterrence against unilateral military attack undertaken outside the United Nations Charter and outside any prior legal authority from the U.N. Security Council or General Assembly.

(h) International law in municipal, national courts: extradition for General Pinochet

A more startling and unexpected demonstration of the new populist-based activism in international law-making was the initiative of a Spanish judge-of-instruction, with the apparent full licence of the Spanish foreign ministry, to proceed in British courts to obtain the extradition of Chilean ex-dictator, General Pinochet, at the time of the action in temporary residence in Great Britain for purposes of undergoing medical treatment. Extradition of General Pinochet to Spain was sought for purposes of trial before the Spanish Courts on the ground of Crimes against Humanity allegedly committed by Pinochet in Chile against persons holding Spanish or double (Spanish and Chilean) nationality. The highest British tribunal, the judicial committee of the House of Lords, in a three-to-two judgment, granted the Spanish request for extradition.[2] The matter then proceeded, on other, non-substantive legal grounds, to further judicial review before the British courts. The original ruling by the British House of Lords, a tribunal not normally noted for venturing on new ground in national or inter-national law, highlighted the fact that, at the end of the twentieth century and the opening of the new Millennium, revolutionary changes are beginning to emerge in International law *doctrines* and jurisprudence, and also in the international law-making processes, balancing the unprecedented changes in international society in the present era of historical transition.

In its final, substantive ruling on the General Pinochet extradition case, the House of Lords, by a 6-to-1 decision, essentially reaffirmed its own earlier ruling, rejecting the Chilean ex-dictator's claims to Sovereign Immunity before British Courts,[3] and ruling that he must remain in Great

24

Britain to face the extradition proceedings from Spain that were based on Crimes against Humanity committed during his *régime* in Chile. In a partial step backwards, the judicial committee of the House of Lords also ruled, however, that Pinochet would not be required to answer in the British extradition proceedings for crimes committed before 1988, the year in which the United Nations Convention on Torture was actually incorporated into British municipal law. While territorially limited in its application to Great Britain, the House of Lords' final ruling appears to herald an end to that *raison d'état* exemption from Criminal Law liability and Criminal Law pursuit that has generally been accorded by national courts to foreign sovereigns and foreign government leaders in respect to acts committed in their own countries against their own or other states' citizens. The British court's final decision thus raises the possibility of a two-track approach to an International Law-based Criminal liability of heads of state or heads of government – the one through municipal, national tribunals and their municipal law which, increasingly, incorporates International Law as part of the law of the land, and the other through international tribunals acting in their own right and directly applying International Law.

Chapter V

ANTINOMIES AND CONTRADICTIONS
IN CONTEMPORARY INTERNATIONAL LAW

The German legal philosopher Radbruch,[1] thought law-making always involved a creative choice among what could be called legal antinomies; not so much jural opposites as characterised by the U.S. legal theorist, Hohfeld, but alternative options as to social or community policy choice in any case. The legal antinomies tended to come, neatly, in pairs, with each policy proposition accompanied by its own antithesis.

(a) The United Nations Charter:
Treaty, or Constitution of World Order?

The complicated political manoeuverings preceding the NATO military alliance's aerial bombardment of Yugoslavia over the Kosovo question involved a by-passing by the United States and its supporting West European states of the United Nations Charter and the United Nations itself as the international institution legally charged with responsibility for maintenance of international peace and security. This seemingly conscious avoidance of the United Nations thus revived a constitutional-legal debate from the early Cold War years. Then, curiously, the political rôles were reversed and it was the United States and its Western bloc supporting states that were championing the cause of a strong United Nations and of a broad, liberal, facultative interpretation of the U.N. Charter. The Soviet Union and the Soviet bloc opposed this approach and argued, instead, for a "limited-treaty" legal characterisation of the U.N organisation and consequently for a restrictive legal interpretation of the U.N. rôles and missions. The dramatically opposing, U.S.-bloc and Soviet-bloc approaches to the United Nations were captured in two very clearly formulated Dissenting Opinions by Soviet bloc judges that were filed in *Certain Expenses of the United Nations*,[2] a 1962 Advisory Opinion of the International Court of Justice rendered in connection with the attempt by the United States, in the U.N. General Assembly, to use Article 19 of the

26

U.N. Charter to deprive the Soviet Union (and also France) of their votes in the U.N. General Assembly because of their failure to pay U.N. special assessments levied against them for purposes of the U.N. peace-keeping operation in the former Belgian Congo. (The Soviet Union and France had both refused to pay the special assessments because, for quite different motives, they each considered that the U.N. Congo operation was being used by the then U.N. Secretary-General Hammarskjold for improper political purposes).

The then Court President Winiarski, a Polish jurist, in his Dissent, set out the fundamentals of the limited-treaty conception of the U.N. Charter:

"The Charter, a multilateral treaty which was the result of prolonged and laborious negotiations, carefully created organs and determined their competence and means of action. The intention of those who drafted it was clearly to abandon the possibility of useful action rather than to sacrifice the balance of carefully established fields of competence ...." [3]

The Soviet Judge on the Court, Judge Koretsky, made the same point even more succinctly in his own Dissent:

"I am prepared to stress the necessity of the strict observation and proper interpretation of the provisions of the Charter, its rules, without limiting itself by reference to the purposes of the Organisation: otherwise one would have to come to the long ago condemned formula: 'The ends justify the means'". [4]

The countervailing intellectual-legal approach to the Winiarski and Koretsky Dissents was that sponsored, in the immediate post-war years, by U.S. jurists and particularly those associated with Professor Myres McDougal of the Yale University Law School. [5] It is best summed up in the celebrated dictum of the great early Chief Justice of the U.S. Supreme Court, John Marshall: "Never forget that it is a constitution that we are expounding."

The immediate post-World War II period was one of great intellectual energy and creativity in U.S. law schools, and also of great faith and optimism in the future of the United Nations and world organisation. It was also a period, – before the full impact of Decolonisation and the admission of a flood of new, former Imperial, Colonial territories into the United Nations – when the U.S. and its bloc members and associates possessed a clear voting majority in the U.N. General Assembly whose member-states did not exceed 60 until late 1955. This flexible, purposive, policy-oriented approach to construction of the powers of the main U.N organs reached its *apogée* with the famous Uniting-for-Peace Resolution, adopted by the U.N General Assembly on 3 November 1950, during the Korean crisis, by a vote of 52 to 5, with 2 abstentions. This innovative, law-making Resolution 377(V) laid down for the first time, as United Nations constitutional law, the legal doctrine that exercise of the legal Veto in the Security Council by any Permanent Member of the Council should not, and in strictly legal terms could not, paralyse the United Nations or relieve the General Assembly of the plentitude of its peace and security powers under the U.N. Charter:

> "If the Security Council, because of lack of unanimity of the permanent members, fails to exercise its primary responsibility for maintenance of international peace and security in any case ... then the General Assembly shall consider the matter immediately with a view to making appropriate recommendations to Members for collective measures, including in the case of a breach of the peace or act of aggression the use of armed force when necessary, to maintain or restore international peace and security."

The U.N. General Assembly-based Uniting-for-Peace strategy had been devised by U.S. President Harry Truman and his Secretary of State, Dean Acheson, to meet the potential threat of a Soviet Veto in the Security Council against any proposed U.N. collective military action to counter, in the case of the divided state of Korea, the invasion of the U.S. bloc-leaning South by the Communist-dominated North. At the time of the original invasion by the North, in June, 1950, the Soviet Union was boycotting the Security Council, in protest against the Security Council's earlier rejection of a Soviet motion not to recognise the credentials of Nationalist China (the then Chinese Government-in-exile in Taiwan). The first U.N. measures to provide military support for South Korea had been able to be voted on and adopted by the Security Council in late June and in July, 1950, in the absence of the Soviet Union and hence the absence of any Soviet Veto. The Soviet Union had, however, resumed its seat in the Security Council on 1 August 1950, and an alternative and legally empowering route for further U.N. action, – through the General Assembly – thus needed to be devised. Hence the Uniting-for-Peace legal stratagem.

With the rapid expansion of the U.N. membership, from the late 1950s on, following on the successive waves of new member-states emerging from the Decolonisation process, a new Third World voting coalition emerged in the General Assembly with an effective voting majority on many key policy issues. The U.S. position on the United Nations and its constitutional powers and their prudent limits began to approximate, increasingly, to that espoused earlier by the Soviet Union. During the developing period of Soviet-U.S. Détente in the 1960s and early 1970s, the two superpowers seemed to prefer to regulate their differences outside the United Nations and its specialised arenas, in direct bilateral diplomacy or bilateral Summit Meetings.

The movement for reform of the United Nations and for amendment of the U.N. Charter accordingly, which preoccupied several successive U.N. Secretaries-General in the 1980s and the early 1990s – Perez de Cuellar and Boutros-Ghali – was spearheaded by states other than the five Permanent Members of the Security Council, and it was directed, principally, at limiting the use (and alleged abuse) of the legal Veto power of the Permanent Members in the Security Council. Not surprisingly, no one of the five Permanent Members of the Security Council gave the assorted reform proposals much encouragement.

The "enemy states" from World War II, excluded by definition from the original United Nations formed at San Francisco in 1945 and subject to the threat of their own special punitive sanctions under Articles 53 and 107 of the U.N. Charter, had soon become, by virtue of their own national industrial rebirths post-war, economic power-houses of the World Community.

In U.N. Security Council-authorised ventures like the Gulf War operation of 1990-1, Germany and Japan were each called on to assume huge portions of the total financial costs of the U.N. operation. It was politically logical and inevitable that they should seek tangible recognition of their new political stature by way of admission to Permanent Member status in the Security Council. This produced, in sequence, demands by other states approaching major power condition by virtue of their population size or their regional-geographical location, for similar treatment. Among such additional geopolitical candidates for Permanent seats on the Security Council were India, Brazil, and Nigeria.

A Special Committee on the Charter of the United Nations and on the Strengthening of the Rôle of the Organisation, appointed by the General Assembly by Resolution in December, 1982, and reporting back within one year, was quite categorical in its criticisms:

"The right of veto had paralysed the Security Council; reforms were needed if the Council was to function effectively.

[Such paralysis] touched upon the credibility of the Security Council and, since criticism of the Security Council's ineffectiveness reflected upon the United Nations, affected that Organisation's image."[6]

However, adding five new Permanent Members to the Security Council to satisfy the claims of the new, economic or geopolitical powers in the World Community was viewed unfavourably by middle-ranking powers – Canada, for example – which viewed any such changes as likely to diminish their own chances of serving on the Security Council with any frequency, in the regular rotation of seats on the Council for non-Permanent Members. Alternative options of simply dramatically increasing the number of seats on the Council, such as had been done, for example, from time to time with the International Law Commission, were viewed with reserve as likely to change the character and effective political rôle of the Council in unpredictable ways. In default of more positive support, lesser suggestions, involving changes in the constitutional customs or practice of exercise of the Veto by the Permanent Members through a "gentleman's agreement"–type of self-restraint, would not necessarily help with "hard cases" like the Gulf War or Kosovo operations. The Amending machinery for the Charter, under Chapter XVIII, Articles 108 and 109, is extremely difficult to operate, for it requires the assent of all the Permanent Members of the Security Council at crucial stages.

U.N. Secretary-General Boutros Boutros-Ghali's own proposals for Charter reform, "An Agenda for Peace", prepared pursuant to a Summit Meeting held by the Security Council at the level of Heads of State and Government, on 31 January 1992, sensibly stayed away from the politically difficult issue of changes to the Security Council on which no consensus had been apparent over the past decade and more during which it had been discussed at the United Nations. The focus, pragmatically, was a functional one, attending to the U.N. responsibilities under the Charter for peace-keeping and peace-making (Chapters VI and VII); and also the capacity for exercise of U.N. diplomacy including measures to build confidence, vastly improved fact-finding, early warning, anticipatory or preventive deployment of U.N. forces in advance of an actual crisis, and the establishment of demilitarised zones. Interesting new elements concerned peace-enforcement units and post-conflict peace-building. Boutros-Ghali's premature departure from the U.N. Security-Generalship after the failure of his bid for a second five-year term apparently put an end to these particular reform initiatives. In November, 1996, the Security Council had voted, 14-to-1, to endorse a second term for Boutros-Ghali, but the one dissenting vote, from the United States, constituted a legal Veto and it was maintained by the U.S. notwithstanding the evident support by the rest of the United Nations for the incumbent Secretary-General. In spite of the departure of Boutros-Ghali and his replacement by one of his principal aides, Kofi Annan, who had been indicated by the U.S. State Department, during the U.N. vote, as fully acceptable to the U.S., the decision was made by the U.S. in the events leading on to the armed intervention against Yugoslavia in March, 1999, to by-pass the United Nations and operate through the former Cold War era, Western military alliance, NATO.

(b) Non-Intervention/Humanitarian Intervention

The claimed International Law doctrine of Humanitarian Intervention is essentially a latter-day creation emerging in the post-World War II era. Brierly had noted that even as late as 1946, in the British Yearbook of International Law, Sir Hersch Lauterpacht, "the great protagonist for the recognition of human rights, felt bound to concede that the doctrine of humanitarian intervention had 'never become a fully acknowledged part of the positive international law'". [7] On the face of it, with the adoption of the United Nations Charter, the doctrine's main protagonists would find a heavy burden of proof cast upon them, in view of the Charter's express interdiction, under Article 2(4), of the threat or use of armed force against the territorial integrity or political independence of any state; and also the Charter's similar express denial, under Article 2(7), of any authority to the United Nations to intervene in matters essentially within the domestic jurisdiction of any state (save only for the special case of enforcement measures authorised by the U.N. itself under Chapter VII of the Charter).

Those who argue today for a doctrine of Humanitarian Intervention usually go back to Classical International Law before the adoption of the U.N. Charter; though the relevance of carrying over Customary law examples from the pre-World War II era to the post-Charter era has to be demonstrated. Most of these asserted Classical, Customary precedents, when examined, turn out to be examples of earlier International Law categories like Retorsion and Reprisals that are now generally considered to have lapsed into desuetude with the adoption of the Charter; or else, like Pacific Blockade, to have been severely limited and confined with the historical evolution of Customary International Law itself. The exaggerated claims, based on diplomatic protection of their own nationals, advanced by European Imperial, Colonial powers in the 19th and early 20th centuries to be able to intervene, by military force, to compel specific performance on various economic development contracts or concessions for the exploitation of natural resources, usually involving Latin American states, have also had to yield to emerging special Latin American or other regional International Law doctrines, sometimes embodied in express bilateral or general regional treaties and accords.

The list of such claimed precursors of a right of Humanitarian Intervention, exercised unilaterally or by a small coterie of "like-minded"' countries, is neither inspiring nor very persuasive in contemporary International Law terms. Uniformly, the examples are Eurocentrist, involving unilateral claims asserted by Western or Western European powers against states outside the family of "subjects" of International Law as defined in Classical International Law. The claims to intervene against the Ottoman Empire – the "unspeakable Turk" in Gladstone's phrase, – were asserted by assorted British Prime Ministers as the excuse for meddling in Balkan politics in the late 19th century.

But the end of the 20th century has even seen assorted Christian groups make a latter-day, well-publicised pilgrimage to the Middle East to "apologise" for the medieval Crusades launched by Christian Western Europe against the "Infidels".

Lord Palmerston, who may have also objected to the then Greek monarch's over-friendly relations with France, had blockaded Greek ports in 1850 in alleged protest over damage to the property of a naturalised British subject from Gibraltar, Don Pacifico, that had occurred during a civil riot in Athens in 1847. Fortunately for the general cause of International Law, Palmerston limited the blockade to Greek ships, thereby acknowledging some reasonably modest limits to the doctrine of Pacific Blockade. When, however, Great Britain, Germany and Italy decided to blockade all the ports of Venezuela in 1902, in alleged protest against damages suffered by their nationals during a civil war, the Germans at first attempted to apply the blockade to the ships of third states as well as of Venezuela; and a German warship, the Panther, engaged in artillery fire against local batteries. Both the Don Pacifico case and the Venezuela blockade eventually went to third party settlement. The positive spin-off from the Venezuela blockade "gunboat diplomacy" was to reinforce the movement in Latin American International Law to deny to European Imperial powers any right of direct, armed intervention, in claimed exercise of the diplomatic protection of their nationals. The earlier corrective, defensive legal actions initiated by Latin American jurists of the late 19th century under the rubric of the Calvo Clause and the Calvo Doctrine, were reinforced by the Venezuela blockade incident. Drawing added intellectual strength from the U.S.-proclaimed Monroe Doctrine which, almost a century earlier, had denied the post-Congress of Vienna Holy Alliance of European powers the right to assert themselves, by military means, over breakaway independence movement in the European colonies in the Americas, the Latin American states, with U.S. Administration support, proclaimed the new Drago Doctrine, later incorporated as part of the Hague Convention of 1907, denying any right on the part of outside states to use armed force for the collection of their own nationals' contract debts. Other aspects of the Drago Doctrine asserted the prior obligation to exhaust all local remedies before appealing to one's country of nationality for legal protection.

The combined military force organised by the European powers to restore their own national interests in China after the Boxer Rebellion of 1900 was also sought to be justified, in legal terms, as an exercise in Humanitarian Intervention. It is not surprising, against this developed historical experience, that the principal political pressures in San Francisco in 1945 for entrenching the principle of Non-Intervention in the United Nations Charter should come from the Latin American states' delegates to the U.N. founding conference. Article 2(7) of the new U.N. Charter was the result. Any legal accommodation between this principle and the new wave of special conventions and U.N. General Assembly Resolutions on human rights would have to come within the U.N. institutional framework and be made compatibly with the U.N. Charter. In view of the prohibition on the Use of Force under Article 2(4) of the Charter, any foreign armed intervention in claimed protection of human rights within another country would require, as specifically allowed under Article 2(7) itself, the prior legal authorisation of a U.N. Security Council Resolution to that effect under Chapter VII of the Charter.

The examples since 1945 of unilateral intervention, without any prior legal authority of the United Nations Security Council, are equally unpromising as claimed precedents for contemporary use of force. They include that particular Cold War legal gloss, established through tacit tolerance, at least, by the two bloc leaders, of what Professor Schwarzenberger identified as Hegemonial Intervention by a bloc leader designed to quell dissidence or dissonance within its own bloc. The Soviet armed interventions in Hungary in 1956 and in Czechoslovakia in 1968 certainly come within this category. One might join with those examples the U.S. intervention in Nicaragua in 1982 against that country's elected government – activities that were to be roundly condemned by the International Court of Justice in its 1986 judgment in Nicaragua v. U.S.[8];

and perhaps the U.S. involvement in the 1961 unsuccessful "Bay of Pigs" operation launched, with covert U.S. support, by Cuban dissidents located in the U.S. against the Castro Government.

(c) Territorial integrity/self determination of peoples

The principle of the territorial integrity of states flowed logically and inevitably from the Treaty of Westphalia in 1648 and its establishment of the nation-state as the master institution of the "modern" system of international relations that was ushered in with the ending of the Thirty Years War. The principle is recognised expressly in Article 2(4) of the United Nations Charter with its legal prohibition of the use of force to promote any change in the territorial status quo of existing frontiers. It is one of the principles of the International Law of Peaceful Coexistence, reaffirmed as such throughout the Cold War and the succeeding period of East-West *Détente*, and triumphantly codified in the United Nations General Assembly's celebrated Resolution of 24 October 1970 approving the Declaration on Principles of International Law concerning Friendly Relations and Cooperation among States in accordance with the Charter of the United Nations (UNGA Resolution 2625 (XXV)). It is an integral element of the Helsinki Final Act of 1975. This is hardly surprising, considering that a principal objective of the Conference on Security and Cooperation in Europe which had launched the Helsinki Final Act as the keystone of the East-West *Détente* process in Europe had always been the recognition and legitimation of the *de facto* territorial settlements that had been agreed upon by the Big Three in the great Wartime conferences at Yalta and elsewhere and established effectively with the military capitulations of 1945. The guarantee of the political-military territorial *status quo* of 1945 was viewed, in strictly military-logistical terms, as the key to maintenance of East-West peace and avoidance of nuclear war, throughout the Cold War and the succeeding era of *Détente*.

Yet in true dialectical fashion the principle of the territorial integrity of states has always marched in tandem, historically, with the principle of self-determination of peoples. Self-determination had been at the core of the triad of principles – liberalism, nationalism, and independence – fostered by the French Revolution and the Napoleonic settlement throughout the 19th century. It had been a rallying call for the popular movements for Italian and German unification and for the challenges to the political unity of the multi-national Habsburg Empire. It was the intellectual inspi-

34

ration for Points 6 to 13 of President Woodrow Wilson's celebrated Fourteen Points as presented to the joint session of the United States Congress on 8 January 1918 as a statement of the U.S. peace plans for the European conflict that the U.S. had entered in the previous year. The German diplomatic Note of 6 October 1918 seeking to open negotiations for an end to the First World War was directly related to a non-punitive peace, without territorial annexations or indemnities, – this on the basis of President Wilson's Fourteen Points. The fact that the United States' European allies had already cynically ignored the Fourteen Points' principles in their own secret wartime agreements, and that the Treaty of Versailles and related peace treaties of 1919, particularly those relating to Eastern Europe, the Balkans, and the Middle East (the Treaties of Saint-Germain, Neuilly, Trianon and Sèvres), all proceeded on classical Imperialist lines of dividing up the spoils of victory, did not alter the Fourteen Points' continuing appeal as part of a new, post-Classical international law.

Within the United Nations in the 1950s and the 1960s, as U.N. membership expanded from the original, overwhelmingly European and Latin American "founders' club" at San Francisco in 1945, self-determination began to take on its own special connotation of Decolonisation and independence of local, indigenous peoples in the overseas Colonial Empires of Western European Imperial states. The political-legal success of this equation of self-determination with the Decolonisation imperative is highlighted in U.N. General Assembly Resolution 1514 (XV) of 14 December 1960 (Declaration on the granting of independence to Colonial countries and peoples), and also in Resolution 1803 (XVII) of 1962 (Declaration on Permanent Sovereignty over Natural Resources); and in subsequent General Assembly and Security Council Resolutions. There was the extra imprimatur of the International Court of Justice Advisory Opinion ruling in *Namibia* in 1971[9], effectively terminating the then White minority-governed Republic of South Africa's League of Nations Mandate over South-West Africa.

In non-Colonial situations, the problems for existing multi-national states having significant ethno-cultural or linguistic minorities within their frontiers offered frequent collisions between the self-determination principle and the principle of the territorial integrity of states and the legitimacy of the territorial *status quo*. The Versailles and dependent World War I Peace Treaties included a regularised system for the protection of racial, linguistic and religious minorities inhabiting the territories of defeated states, – Austria, Hungary, Bulgaria and Turkey. States belonging to the victorious Allied coalition, like Yugoslavia, Romania and Greece, and new, succession states like Poland and Czechoslovakia, concluded special treaties with similar obligations of protection of minorities. Germany and Poland adopted a special bilateral convention on Upper Silesia. What might be called an overarching League of Nations-based system of legal protection of national minorities, in operation in Europe from 1919 until 1932, rested upon guarantees under municipal law which could not be changed by ordinary law; and upon International Law-based Guarantee Treaties whose provisions could only be changed with the approval of the Council of the League of Nations, with disputes between states over the application of the Treaties being subject to the Compulsory Jurisdiction of the Permanent Court of International Justice. This Court's jurisdiction was in fact actively invoked, leading to a number of important Court rulings.[10] The League system, which had also seen popular plebiscites and international Mixed Commissions, came to an end, effectively, with the rise of pathological nationalism in the early 1930s, leading on to World War II.

In the immediate post-World War II era, the self-determination principle was legally conditioned and confined by the wartime agreements of the Allied, Big Three powers, especially at Yalta in February, 1945, and in the Postsdam Agreement of August, 1945, made after Germany's unconditional surrender. These agreements sanctioned the compulsory transfer of people from the German provinces now lost because of Yalta and Potsdam and also, from pre-War Poland and from Czechoslovakia and from Hungary. The confused events on the termination of hostilities in Europe in May, 1945, included the flight of civil populations in fear of physical danger, and also arbitrary expulsions without any adequate transfer administration and without compensation. The estimates of the total populations involved in the mass flights and expulsions range up to 14 million, with loss of life of up to 2 million. This was a precursor of what, in the 1990s, was to become characterised as "ethnic cleansing", and as incompatible with a fundamental right to one's homeland (Recht auf der Heimat). It was not, of course, the first example. Under the Lausanne Peace Treaty and the Greek-Turkish Agreement of 1923 on exchange of minorities, $1\frac{1}{2}$ million ethnic Greeks of Turkish nationality had been forced to leave Asia Minor or, having already fled during the military hostilities, had been prevented from returning home; while 400,000 ethnic Turks of Greek nationality had been obliged to leave Greece and settle in Turkey.

The British Foreign Secretary, Lord Curzon, had warned, at the time, of the dangers of establishing a precedent, in International Law, for forcible transfers of populations, though the Lausanne Treaty had provided for an international mixed commission to supervise the population exchanges and property liquidations involved. The legal issues were partly clarified by an Advisory Opinion of the Permanent Court of International Justice in 1926.[11] But Lord Curzon's concern remains. Should not even internationally authorised and supervised population transfers and exchanges, unless they are genuinely voluntary and evidenced as such (by prior, popular plebiscite vote, for example), be treated as expulsions and, as such, as being in violation of International Law?

With the ending of the Cold War, existing multi-national states face a revival of nationalism and ethnic-cultural fractionalism of the sort common throughout the 19th century and up to and including the two World Wars, but temporarily held in check by the Cold War's Bipolar system of World public order with its Metternichean consequence and emphasis on maintaining internal order and the political status quo within each of the rival blocs. Plural-constitutional states, like Canada, might try earnestly and not perhaps always completely successfully, to reconcile claims to particularised constitutional protection of ethno-cultural distinctness within the confines of a classical, Westminster-model, federal system that normally emphasises constitutional equality of treatment to its constituent, geographically-based units. Hitherto unitary states like Great Britain may experiment today with devolution of essentially local powers to new regional assemblies. Such efforts are of course a reflex of the diametrically different trends in contemporary, post-Cold War constitutionalism: the centripetal trend towards supra-national political and economic integration and ultimately legal union on the one hand, and the centrifugal trend towards large-scale devolution and decentralisation of decision-making power within a state. It is apparent that current initiatives towards creating more decentralised, pluralistic federal structures encounter enormous practical and also scientific-legal difficulties in responding to the revival of nationalism and also, in certain cases, to the emergence of a constitutional identity for indigenous aboriginal peoples who may, previously, have been constitutionally neglected or ignored. The practical reconciliation of federalism with the new claims of self-determination of peoples within an existing state, as a constitutional-legal alternative to outright secession or political breakaway, may require somewhat more imaginative constitutional thinking and the development of new, flexible models for plural constitutionalism in place of the too rigid and legalistic, Classical, Westminster stereotypes. That is quite a challenge to legal imagination and innovation, of course. It should not be forgotten that a major preoccupation of the negotiation teams of Canada, the Soviet Union and some others

37

in the marathon sessions of the U.N. General Assembly Special Committee that drafted the celebrated Declaration on the International Law of Friendly Relations, of October, 1970, was to ensure the non-applicability of its proclaimed International Law right of self-determination of peoples to the situation of existing federal states.

(d) Non-Use-of-Force/Collective (Regional) Self Defence

The legal starting point today must be the definition of the purposes and principles of the United Nations, set out in the opening Article of the U.N. Charter:

"Chapter I. Purposes and Principles
Article 1. The Purposes of the United Nations are:
To maintain international peace and security, and to that end: to take effective collective measures for the prevention and removal of threats to the peace, and for the suppression of acts of aggression or other breaches of the peace."

The follow-up Article, Article 2, both establishes the paramount obligation of all Members of the United Nations to "settle their international disputes by peaceful means", (Article 2^1); and also reiterates the principle of the Non-Use-of-Force (Article 2^4): -

"All Members shall refrain in their international relations from the threat or use of force against the territorial integrity or political independence of any state, or in any other manner inconsistent with the Purposes of the United Nations."

Chapter V of the U.N. Charter (the Security Council), confers on the Security Council "primary responsibility for the maintenance of international peace and security" (Article 24^1); but stipulates that, in carrying out this responsibility, the Security Council will act in accordance with the purposes and principles of the United Nations, Chapters VI, VII, and VIII of the Charter being specifically cited (Article 24^2).

Chapter VI of the Charter (Pacific Settlement of Disputes) is the part under which the special gloss of U.N. Peace-keeping was developed, with its sanctioning of the use of unarmed military personnel drawn from U.N. member-countries who would, literally, interpose themselves between parties to an international or internal, civil conflict that had already agreed to a military cease-fire and that were looking for some diplomatic and political face-saving way out of their impasse. U.N Peace-keeping was devised by then Canadian Foreign Minister and later Prime Minister, Lester Pearson, in the Suez Canal crisis of 1956, to facilitate an ending of hostilities by allowing the British and French to withdraw their invading armed forces from the Suez Canal zone as elegantly as possible, after the U.S. Administration had indicated it would withdraw financial support for the Pound Sterling and French Franc if the British and French governments did not immediately desist from their armed intervention. U.N. Peacekeeping under Chapter VI was applied thereafter, with varying degrees of success, to the former Belgian Congo in 1960, after a too rapid last-minute decolonisation by Belgium had bought about regional secession and civil war; and it was applied in other later armed conflicts around the World. Usually, the U.N Peace-keeping force would be constituted on an ethno-culturally, regionally representative and balanced basis, with three different national forces making up the total U.N. force. Middle-rank states that were not considered to be too strongly involved in the Cold War ideological battles of the times were selected, with states like India, Poland, and Canada tending to recur as components of such U.N forces.

Chapter VII of the U.N. Charter (Action with respect to Threats to the Peace, Breaches of the Peace, and Acts of Aggression) provides the legal base for what is now characterised as U.N. Peace-*making* – the actual utilisation of armed force by U.N. or U.N.-authorised personnel, in fulfillment of the purposes and principles of the U.N. Charter, under the authority of prior U.N. Security Council Resolutions specially adopted in that behalf. Article 39 provides that the Security Council shall – "determine the existence of any threat to the peace, breach of the peace, or act of aggression", and make recommendations accordingly for collective U.N. action under Articles 41 and 42 of the Charter to maintain or restore international peace and security.

Article 41 specifies measures not involving the use of armed force, including – "complete or partial interruption of economic relations and of rail, sea, air, postal, telegraphic, radio, and other means of communication, and the severance of diplomatic relations." Article 42 allows the Security Council, if it considers such Article 41 measures (not involving the use of armed force) to be "inadequate or to have proved inadequate", to take "such action by air, sea, or land forces as may be necessary to maintain or restore international peace and security."

To Article 42 we must add Article 51 which contains both an additional affirmative legal support for collective armed action under Charter auspices and also a potentially troubling exemption to the Non-Use-of-Force principle:

"Nothing in the present Charter shall impair the inherent right of individual or collective self-defence if an armed attack occurs against a Member of the United Nations, until the Security Council has taken measures necessary to maintain international peace and security."

Articles 42 and 51, taken together, provided the full legal authority for the United Nations collective action for the maintenance of international peace and security in the Korean crisis of 1950, when a multi-national force, operating under the U.N. aegis and commanded by a U.S. General operating under U.N. authority, was formed after a military invasion of South Korea was made by North Korean forces in the territorially divided state created by the Yalta accords and the *de facto* settlement of the War in Asia in August, 1945. The collective security action by the United Nations in the Korean crisis provided an additional legal gloss on the U.N. Charter of a Charter-related legal authority for the U.N. General Assembly to act to fill any gaps in U.N. law-making on peace-making that might result from the use of the Veto in the Security Council by any one of its Permanent Members. This was the Uniting-for-Peace Resolution, Resolution 377(V), sponsored by U.S. President Truman and Secretary of State Dean Acheson, and adopted by the General Assembly on 23 November 1950, by a vote of 52 to 5 with 2 abstentions. It provided a necessary alternative legal base for U.N. collective action, after the Soviet Union, which had chosen to absent itself from the Security Council at the time the first, U.N.-empowering Resolutions on the Korean crisis were adopted by the Security Council in June 1950, had changed its position and returned to its Permanent seat on the Security Council.

Articles 42 and 51 were, again, the legal authority for U.N. collective security action in the Gulf War crisis of 1990-1, after Iraq had invaded Kuwait in order to produce a military solution to long-standing frontier disputes between the two states. The mode of U.N. operation as to Kuwait was different, however, to the Korean War model. Instead of one or two master U.N. Resolutions, there was a continuing series of Resolutions which, taken together, provided an overarching, umbrella legal authority. And the overall military command of the U.N.-authorised multi-national action in restoration of Kuwait territorial integrity was entrusted to a U.S. General reporting directly to the U.S. President rather than to the U.N. There had been no difficulty in rallying substantial support within the United Nations in support of the collective action against Iraq. Thirty states, including key Arab states of the region, joined in the collective action, with nineteen of these apparently taking part in combatant activity. Other states with a long history of voluntary engagement in Chapter VI (U.N. Peace-*keeping*) rather than Chapter VII (U.N. Peace-making) activities, seem to have limited themselves to logistical support action not involving the direct application of armed force or combat operations. When President Clinton proposed, in 1996, follow-up armed action against Iraq for its alleged non-compliance with the 1991 Gulf War military cease-fire terms, no new U.N. Security Council legal authority was forthcoming and reliance had to be placed upon the old bundle of Resolutions from 1990-1. Only the U.S. and the former League of Nations Mandatory power, Great Britain, took part in the 1996 operation.

In the early-1999 phase of the decade-long, continuing crisis of Yugoslav State Succession, because of a stated fear and expectation of a Russian or Chinese Veto in the Security Council, no approach to obtain legal authority in behalf of collective security action against the rump Yugoslav state was ever made to the U.N. Security Council. Nor, surprisingly, was any approach made to the U.N. General Assembly where, of course, no Veto could apply, and this in spite of the fact that the main sponsor of the armed intervention against Yugoslavia was the U.S. State Department which could hardly have been unaware of the alternative constitutional-legal route of a General Assembly-based legal authority, on the precedent of the Korean War Uniting-for-Peace Resolution initiated by the U.S. President and the U.S. Secretary of State of that earlier era. In default of Security Council or General Assembly prior legal authority for the application of armed force against Yugoslavia in 1999, recourse had to be made, *faute de mieux*, to either Chapter VIII of the Charter (Regional Arrangements), or to Chapter VII, Article 51 (collective self-defence), with the Cold War vestigial military alliance, NATO, as the vehicle for any such action. Chapter VIII is not, in its language and terms, particularly helpful. It commences (Article 52(1)) with an apologetic, "saving" clause: "Nothing in the present Charter precludes the existence of regional arrangements or agencies for dealing with such matters relating to the maintenance of international peace and security as are appropriate for regional action";

But it then adds the limiting qualification –

"provided that such arrangements or agencies and their activities are consistent with the Purposes and Principles of the United Nations."

And while the Security Council may, – "where appropriate, utilise such regional arrangements or agencies for enforcement action under its authority", (Article 53(1)), it is expressly stipulated in the same Article that:

"no enforcement action shall be taken under regional arrangements or by regional agencies without the authorisation of the Security Council"

The only exceptions to this latter prohibition are the presumably now defunct "enemy states" clauses of the U.N. Charter, whereby, under Article 53 itself and also Article 107, the general interdiction of the use of force in the Charter is expressly waived in the case of Germany and Japan and other losers in World War II.

Chapter VIII (Regional Arrangements) is thus a thin reed on which to lean, legally, to justify any hostile military operations against another state or states that have not already been expressly authorised by a prior Resolution of the Security Council (or by the General Assembly) in terms of Chapter VII of the Charter (U.N. Peace-*making*); or that cannot, by any process of benign interpretation, be brought, literally and in terms, within the quite precisely and restrictively drafted "inherent right of individual or collective self-defence" established under Chapter VII's last Article, Article 51. The initiatives at expanding the Article 51, self-defence exception to the U.N. Charter's general legal prohibition on the Use of Force, through progressive, generic, or "policy" interpretations, have all focussed, more or less exclusively, on an asserted special Cold War gloss – a claimed right of anticipatory, collective self-defence. Its principal protagonist, Julius Stone[12], had cited the hypothetical scenario of a Cold War rival with inter-continental ballistic missiles, armed with nuclear warheads that were ready and activated and about to be launched. Would the intended victim-state be required, under the special International Law of the U.N. Charter, to wait until the hostile missiles had actually been fired and were, presumably, mere seconds away from reaching their target, before taking preventive measures? That particular case-scenario was, fortunately, never encountered concretely during the Cold War period. In fact, the Kennedy-Khrushchev ultimate peaceful resolution of the Cuban Missile crisis in October, 1962, spawned special preventive, protective counter-measures such as the emergency Hot-line, Red-line, direct telephone communication between the White House and the Kremlin to minimise chances of an East-West nuclear conflagration occurring by accident or mistake or misunderstanding. Anticipatory collective self-defencee may be considered to have lapsed into history now with the end of the Cold War. No further scientific-legal attempts at expanding or re-writing the Self-Defence exception have emerged. Article 51 is, for obvious enough political reasons, very precisely drafted so as to minimise any evasion from the Charter prohibition on the Use of Force without the prior authority of the United Nations Security Council. The exercise of the "inherent right of collective self-defense" under s.51 is also expressly conditioned by the necessity of an armed attack already having occurred against a Member of the United Nations. Further, the time duration of such a claimed right of collective self-defense can only extend "until the Security Council has taken measures to maintain international peace and security". Measures taken in the exercise of this claimed right of collective self-defense have to be reported immediately to the Security Council and cannot in any way affect the authority and responsibility of the Security Council under the Charter to take at any time such action as it deems necessary to maintain or restore international peace or security.

NATO, as a claimed regional security organisation, could neither claim nor exercise any enforcement powers in the name of international peace and security except as expressly authorised by the Charter and through the relevant U.N. law-making institutions, the Security Council and the General Assembly. It could have no inherent legal powers in its own name, separately from the Charter, to apply armed force. It could not hoist itself, literally by its own boot-straps, into legal powers that it did not have under the U.N. Charter.

The choice of NATO as the vehicle for the U.S.-led intervention and application of armed force against Yugoslavia was, in itself, unusual. NATO was conceived and developed, in the very earliest, dangerous days of the Cold War when Stalin was still in power in the Soviet Union, as a purely defensive, political-military alliance and association of "like-minded states", brought together by their then common fear of Soviet aggression and their felt need to establish a military counterweight sufficient to deter the Soviet Union from military adventurism in an era of nuclear weapons, and also sufficient to contain the Soviet Union within its then de facto political frontiers flowing from the military cease-fires in Europe and in Asia in 1945 and the earlier, Yalta accords of the same year. Under NATO's auspices, the Western bloc's politic of deterrence and containment *vis-à-vis* the Soviet Union and Soviet bloc had clearly worked. It had soon ripened, under the influence of emerging theories and practice of East-West inter-bloc Peaceful Coexistence and the United Nation's own concept of Friendly Relations, into an International Law of Détente, with inter-bloc mutual accommodations and give-and-take and an essential inter-bloc acceptance of the East-West political-military status quo at War's end in 1945.

It is a tribute to the remarkable group of early leaders of NATO, both civilian Secretaries-General like Lord Ismay and Paul-Henri Spaak, and also Supreme Allied Commanders like General Eisenhower and General Ridgeway, who had all experienced World War II at first hand in operational command positions, that they succeeded in using the Western collective military power to help maintain peace between the two great competing blocs of the era of Bipolarity, without ever escalating into the use, or threat of use, of nuclear weapons. With the exception of their intervention, under clear and unequivocal U.N.-derived legal authority, in the Korean War, which may have been blundered into, on the Soviet Communist side (the People's Republic of China of the 1950s still being allied to the Soviet Union) through error or misjudgment as to Western bloc intentions, the early Western leaders of NATO exercised an exemplary economy in the use of power. The Western alliance had recourse, at all times, to the more moderate forms of control in crisis situations – as in the case of the Cuban Missile crisis of October, 1962, where the Khrushchev-Kennedy eventual mutual accommodation still stands as a text-book example of use of peaceful, non-coercive, diplomatic methods to resolve international tension-issues. General Eisenhower, the leader of the victorious World War II coalition and NATO's first Supreme Commander before he resigned to run successfully for the U.S. Presidency in 1952, drew on his own past direct military experience and his accumulated military-political wisdom to eschew the use of tactical nuclear weapons in support of the French at Dienbienphu in 1954, though that particular course had been counselled to him by his Secretary of State, John Foster Dulles.

With the end of the Cold War, symbolised by the fall of the Berlin Wall in 1989, NATO's military and political *raison d'être* as a Western defensive alliance to contain Soviet Communist military power rapidly disappeared. It had already been ebbing away gradually, over the years, as the Cold War progressively had given way to *Détente*. This was reflected over the years of Détente, in the calibre and character of the succession of different civilian Secretaries-General and military Supreme Commanders of NATO. Faced with the alternative of a "sunset law" that would enable NATO to be wound up altogether now that its original purposes had been fulfilled, the NATO bureaucracy, civilian and military, began the search for new, post-Cold War *rôles* and missions to justify a continued existence. One suggested opening was to expand membership eastward in Europe by bringing in to NATO membership former member-states of COMECON and of the old NATO rival, Warsaw Pact Alliance that had broken away from the Communist system and installed new, non-Communist or at least coalition governments since the fall of the Berlin Wall in 1989. Becoming admitted to NATO would come to be seen as a useful stepping-stone strategy for Eastern and South-Eastern European states seeking entry into the European Union and the European financial and trading community generally. Thus Poland, Hungary, and the Czech Republic were happy to be formally accepted in NATO on March 12, 1999, with NATO itself thus expanding from 16 to 19 members and with its original, Eastern defensive border with the Soviet bloc of the Cold War era thus moving even further eastward to the borders of Russia itself. The three new NATO member-states may, however, have been less than joyful at discovering, a bare two weeks later when the U.S.-led NATO coalition launched its high-level aerial bombardment against Yugoslavia, that they would be expected, as NATO allies now, to rally to the NATO armed attack in the Balkans in concrete ways. Existing NATO allies like Greece resolved the political dilemma, in part, by a conscious dragging of feet. Greece allowed NATO land forces to use the northern Greek port of Thessaloniki for transshipment of personnel and war material on the way to Yugoslavia, but imposed conditions requiring that it all be done at night, in darkness, so as not to exacerbate the local, Greek population which disapproved of the NATO bombings of civilian targets and resulting civilian casualties in Yugoslavia. Hungary seems to have successfully demurred at allowing passage of NATO land forces through its own territories into Yugoslavia, the most direct point of entry. The evident concerns and misgivings among new and old NATO member-states as to reconciling NATO's attack on Yugoslavia with the original, purely defensive purpose of NATO which NATO's own Charter makes explicit, were no doubt compounded by the demonstration, as the aerial bombardment campaign unfolded, of some weaknesses in the NATO leadership, and of failures by NATO civil and military personnel, too long accustomed to Cold War and *Détente* East-West accommodations, to adapt to new strategic-military realities of the post-Cold War era. Was it the civilian or the military leadership of NATO that gave the original advice to the Foreign Ministers of the NATO member-states that one week of high-level aerial bombardment, with "smart bombs", would produce a Yugoslav surrender? Was it, again, the civilian or the military leadership of NATO that failed to warn the NATO Foreign Ministers of the need to establish an adequate base, in International Law, as authority for a NATO attack on Yugoslavia, which, in the absence of a Security Council or General Assembly enabling Resolution, would seem in direct conflict with Article 2(4) of the Charter and the Non-Use-of-Force principle? There remained the impression that no one at NATO headquarters, civilian or military, took the time to call in the Legal Adviser and seek counsel on the issue. That would be a pity, since the past record of Western decision-making in international crisis-situations, throughout the Cold War era and the later period of Détente, was one where the Legal Adviser was constantly present and participating in the process of problem-solving. President Kennedy's rôle in the Cuban Missile crisis, and the crucial part played in that by the State Department's then Legal Adviser, Abe Chayes, in guiding the final choices as to means of conflicts-resolution into the alternative, more moderate controls that would be fully compatible with International Law, in preference to more dramatic and dangerous exercises in flinging down the gauntlet, have been fully chronicled by legal and diplomatic historians and stand today as a continuing precedent and model for peaceful settlement of international disputes.

(e) Bellum justum: Aerial bombardment of civilian targets/ temperamenta belli

The debate over the legality of the NATO use of armed force against Yugoslavia without the authority of a prior, enabling Resolution of the United Nations Security Council or the General Assembly under Chapter VII of the U.N. Charter, has tended to throw into the background another key International Law question. It was not the U.S. President but the British Prime Minister who chose publicly to invoke for the military action against Yugoslavia the philosophical-legal mantle of a Just War. The British Prime Minister did not acknowledge an ultimate theological source in St. Thomas Aquinas and never, in any case, moved on to examine the concrete adaptation and also the intellectual legal refinements of that doctrine introduced by Hugo Grotius and later generations of thinkers on International Law. Is it enough, for example, to invoke the claim of a Just War in behalf of one's own cause, without considering the further, logically sequential issue, of the actual means used to vindicate, in action, that claim of a Just War. May not the postulated justness of the original purpose of a war become diminished or even destroyed by unjustness in the military means and other methods used to carry it out? Grotius' legal writings had recognised the potential legal antinomy between ends and means, with Grotius' development of the concept of *temperamenta belli*, a prime source of so much of today's International Law of War and of the emerging new International Humanitarian Law. The conflict between NATO ends and objectives (presuming now, for purposes of argument, their legal validity),

46

and NATO means, was brought into the open, throughout the Kosovo action, when the porte-parole of NATO, a civilian public relations official, appeared nightly on international television networks to explain the NATO aerial bombardment strategy. It was to be, as the U.S. President had promised at the outset, a "war without casualties", which, more specifically, meant a war without casualties on the NATO alliance side, and this promise was certainly kept as far as the NATO military personnel were concerned except for several pre-hostilities training accidents. From this politically-imposed imperative of the NATO military strategy flowed the decision to limit NATO action to high level aerial bombardment, using "smart bombs" and other postulated fool-proof new combat devices. The NATO *porte-parole's* television *rôle* stemmed from the necessity publicly to defend originally unforeseen consequences of the high-level aerial bombardments that were the substance of the NATO military action. Among these consequences were the destruction of international bridges across the Danube and the resulting interruption or cessation of commercial traffic on the Danube, by riparian states, both members and non-members of the NATO Alliance. This was done although free of passage throughout the Danube had been guaranteed under International Law treaties and other binding international legal arrangements going back well over a century. More serious in human as well as legal terms were the bombardments of convoys of unarmed refugees, of civilian hospitals, of public amenities like the water and electricity services, and not least of the Chinese Embassy in Belgrade. The NATO public response was to say it was all an accident, and to express NATO regrets. A *mea culpa* when offered and offered speedily, is certainly to be welcomed. It could hardly, in itself, however, constitute an effective *ex post facto* legal dispensation from Customary International Law obligations as to *temperamenta belli* in relation to civilian populations; or, more immediately, provide a legal release from the very specific injunctions and limitations on aerial bombardment created by contemporary International Law acts of the nature of the Protocols Additional to the Geneva Conventions of 1949, and specifically Protocol I on Protection of Victims of International Armed Conflict, which were adopted as recently as 1977.

The legality of aerial bombardment when directed against civilian targets as a deliberate instrument of mass terror and an inducement to civil populations to compel their political leaders to surrender had become a burning issue for International Law after the *Luftwaffe* had devastated Guernica in aid of General Franco's rebel forces during the Spanish Civil War in 1937. The *Luftwaffe* attack on Coventry in the early phase of World

47

War II might have been considered to be in the same category. Nonetheless, aerial bombardment was not pursued by the Allied prosecutors of the principal German civil and military leaders at the Nuremberg War Crimes Tribunal in 1946, apparently because of concerns that it might invite comparisons with Allied aerial strategy directed against German targets during the saturation bombing of German cities in the later years of the War. Such Allied attacks might perhaps have been able to be justified, legally, under the doctrine of Reprisal, as a response to the German *Blitzkrieg* against Coventry. The principle of Proportionality remains a limiting legal factor to Reprisal, in the same way that it is also incorporated into the doctrine of *temperamenta belli* and the Law of War generally.

The 1977 Protocols Additional to the Geneva Conventions of 1949 deal directly and in terms with the issues involved in aerial bombardment. Part IV (Civilian Population), Section I (General Protection against effects of hostilities), establishes in its Article 48 (Basic rule): "the Parties to the conflict shall at all times distinguish between the civilian population and combatants and between civilian objects and military objectives and accordingly shall direct their operations only against military objectives".

The concrete follow-up to this is Article 51(2): "The civilian population as such, as well as individual civilians, shall not be the object of attack. Acts or threats of violence the primary purpose of which is to spread terror among the civilian populations are prohibited."
Under Article 51(4): "Indiscriminate attacks are prohibited.
   "Indiscriminate attacks are:
   – those which are not directed at a specific military objective;
   – those which employ a method or means of combat which cannot be directed at a specific military objective; or
   – those which employ a method or means of combat the effects of which cannot be limited as required by this Protocol; and consequently, in each such case, are of a nature to strike military objectives and civilians or civilian objects without distinction."

Article 51 also covers the issue of what was referred to, in the Gulf War 1990-1, under the euphemistic qualification of "collateral damage". This concept was invoked by the NATO *porte-parole* in legal minimisation of the "accidental" bombing of civilian and non-military targets during the NATO action against Yugoslavia.

Article 51(5): "... the following types of attacks are to be considered as indiscriminate:

(a)an attack by bombardment by any methods or means which treats as a single military object a number of clearly separated and distinct military objectives located in a city, town or village or other area containing a similar concentration of civilians or civilian objects; and

(b)an attack which may be expected to cause incidental loss of civilian life, injury to civilians, damage to civilian objects, or a combination thereof, which would be excessive in relation to the concrete and direct military advantage anticipated."

Article 51(6): "Attacks against the civilian population or civilians by way of reprisals are prohibited."

The effect of the 1977 Protocols Additional to the Geneva Conventions of 1949 upon the contemporary International Law of War and upon the Law of aerial bombardment in particular, was raised during the Gulf War 1990-1, when one of the supposedly "smart bombs" launched from the air against the Iraqi capital, Baghdad, evidently went astray or was misdirected by its operators and hit a civilian target, with resultant considerable civilian casualties. Aerial bombardment was not, however, the sole or even the primary Allied military strategy directed against Iraq during the Gulf War. President Bush, operating under the umbrella legal authority of the series of U.N. Security Council Resolutions, was always committed to a ground campaign with U.S. ground forces. The high-level aerial strikes seem to have been phased out after the "smart bombs" mistake, and President Bush, on the advice of the U.S. military commander, General Colin Powell, called a halt to the whole campaign once the stated initial purpose of a withdrawal of the invading Iraqi forces from Kuwait had been achieved. Neither Iraq nor the United States had adhered to the 1977 Protocols, though the general doctrinal-legal view remained that the Protocols' rules were a codification of Customary International Law rules as they had evolved during and after World War II and that, as such, they were binding on signatories and non-signatories alike to the Protocols. The United States, in an earlier, 1987, aerial incident flowing from the Iraq-Iran armed conflict of the 1980s, had been sued before the International Court of Justice by the Iranian Government for the shooting down, by a U.S. warship operating in the Persian Gulf, of an Iranian civilian passenger aircraft operating on a regularly scheduled international commercial passenger flight. The shooting down of the commercial passenger aircraft, with substantial loss of life of the Iranian civilian passengers and air crew, stemmed from a "mistake" on the part of inexperienced U.S. naval personnel who evidently mistook the blip on the radar screen of a slow-moving civil aircraft for an oncoming hostile missile. Smart bombs and smart missiles depend, in the end, on the professional training and experience of those using them. After some considerable delays, the Iran-U.S. conflict was settled out of Court with the Iranian Government withdrawing the suit in return for what is believed to have been a substantial indemnity payment by the U.S. Government.[13]

In the aftermath of the NATO aerial bombardment of Kosovo, a group of private, non-governmental lawyers in the West is reported to have asked the Special Prosecutor of the U.N.'s *ad hoc* War Crimes Tribunal for Yugoslavia to institute a prosecution against individual Heads of Government of NATO member-states, on the score of alleged breaches of the Law of War in the armed action against Yugoslavia, including the Law of aerial bombardment. Such a legal testing could be effected by having the NATO Secretary-General and Supreme Commander, as the civilian and military heads of the military alliance, named as the nominal defendants to a legal process before the Tribunal. The larger International Law issues, however, would seem to be best raised and ruled upon in a reference by the United Nations to the International Court of Justice for an Advisory Opinion ruling on the contemporary International Law principles and rules involved.

(f) World Rule of Law:
Universal jurisdiction/municipal jurisdiction

The term World Rule of Law,[14] has a normative-ambiguity that cloaks the fact that different people and groups use it for quite different purposes. In the late 1940s and the 1950s, it was the call-for-action of a group of intellectual lawyers associated with the American Bar Association as a spin-off from the "One World" paradigm put forward during the War years as the model for the post-War public order system. Building on early, highly idealistic conceptions of the rôle of the new United Nations system, legal thinkers like Grenville Clark and Louis Sohn went on to develop more detailed and concrete, secondary principles. The particular aspect of the World Rule of Law as an overarching idea transcending or uniting the different legal cultures of the World, was lost in the rapid transition from the 1945 victors' consensus to the Cold War and the Bipolar system of World public order and the twin, competing political-military blocs on which that rested.

A different current of legal activity, which temporarily converged with the World Rule of Law movement, was the drive towards international criminal-delictual liability of states and states' governments and their officials, and to its institutionalisation in some form of general or universal international criminal jurisdiction. Rafael Lemkin, the exiled Polish jurist who taught briefly at the Yale Law School in the late 1940s and was, at the same time, a persistent and forceful lobbyist at the United Nations and its new Human Rights Division, launched the, at the time, novel International Law category of Genocide, as a crime transcending existing municipal, national law norms and that, being employed so often as an instrument of state, governmental policy, effectively escaped the control of municipal criminal law. Though Lemkin himself never formulated a programmatic, institutionalised application of the postulated new international crime of Genocide, the call for a permanent International Criminal Court flowed logically and inevitably from his idea.

At the Nuremberg War Crimes Tribunal, set up by the victorious wartime allies to put on trial and prosecute and judge and finally condemn the political and military leaders of defeated Nazi Germany, the most interesting count from the legal viewpoint was the new charge of Crimes against Humanity. Prosecution for breaches of the Law of War, much of which was still Customary International Law, had been proposed by the victors of the earlier, First World War, 1914-1918, but left, in its practical implementation, to the countries of nationality of the alleged perpetrators, with indifferent or inconclusive results. The national judges concerned with the resultant national trials for breaches of the Law of War seem to have concluded, quietly, that the criminal liability principle was one-sided if only the defeated states were seen as obligated to apply it to their nationals. While another count at Nuremberg, the Crime of Aggressive War, had "One World" legal associations and also trans-national historical legal roots going back to the Kellogg-Briand Pact of 1928, its application at Nuremberg might be seen to be impaired by the fact that it was interpreted and enforced by a tribunal whose judges were all selected from the victor states, with neutral states and *a fortiori* the defeated Axis states not being represented on the tribunal. Unofficial approaches were known to have been made to well-known jurists from neutral states in World War II to see if they might agree to serve on the Nuremberg tribunal but they had, after consultation, with their own national foreign ministries, declined to become involved.

The central dilemma inherent in the Kellogg-Briand Pact of 1928 of

51

how, if you outlaw the recourse to war as an instrument of national policy, you are to go about producing change in International Law and the international society it is supposed to reflect, had been attempted to be resolved in the Covenant of the League of Nations, with its provision in Article 19 (Review of Treaties) authorising the Assembly of the League to advise reconsideration of treaties which had become inapplicable and, in the same context, to examine international conditions whose continuance might endanger peace. Article 19 of the Covenant was, however, never seriously approached as a vehicle for peacefully adjusting the World public order system to rapidly changing political and societal conditions in the World Community of the inter-War period. The one major area in which timely peaceful adjustment of a treaty might have obviated or mitigated subsequent pathological pressures for change, was the case of the Austro-German Customs Union where the Permanent Court of International Justice, in 1931,[15] by narrow margin, refused to allow consensual readjustment of the Versailles Treaty settlements' stipulations on the status of Austria.

For the thoroughly new count at the Nuremberg Tribunal of 1946, Crimes against Humanity, ultimate legal sources had to be found, if at all, in large and necessarily rather vague philosophical-legal concepts like the canons of Natural Law; or a little more empirically, perhaps, in notions of a latter-day *Jus Gentium* and of elemental principles of law common to all mature legal systems – what the Statute of the World Court, in 1920, had identified, in its Article 38(c), as "the general principles of law recognised by civilised nations." And yet, in spite of the virtual absence of settled international jurisprudence, international judicial decisions, or even international *doctrines* of the sort identified by Article 38(d) of the World Court Statute as "the teachings of the most highly qualified publicists of the various nations", the Crimes Against Humanity count at the Nuremberg Tribunal seems to have been the most lasting in terms of its general public acceptance as transcending "victors' justice", and also because of its claims to universality on a comparative law basis.

The subsequent extreme political difficulties in making the progression from an essentially *ad hoc*, one-shot tribunal like the Nuremberg tribunal created and staffed by the victors in an armed conflict, to a permanent, standing international tribunal which would draw on all states in the World Community without, at the same time, any special legal rights or privileges or status for victor states, must remain a major disappointment in the progressive development of International Law since World War II. The superpowers and the other Permanent Members of the U.N. Security

52

Council have proved the most determined and also the most powerful politically of the opponents of a general international criminal liability and of a genuinely universal jurisdiction and competence to deal with alleged breaches of International Law norms and rules. The political culmination, in July, 1998, of the campaign to establish a permanent International Criminal tribunal, with the adoption of the Rome Statute of the International Criminal Court, was marred by certain political facts-of-life. To enter into legal force, the Statute will have to be ratified by 60 states, a significant increase in the number of necessary parties over, for example, the Ottawa Land Mines Treaty adopted in 1997. More seriously, however, it was indicated by the state diplomatic representatives involved that the Statute would not now be ratified by the United States or apparently, also, by at least three of the other four Permanent Members of the U.N. Security Council. The objections on the part of those states are not a legal barrier to adoption of the Statute, which will take effect as soon as the minimum number of 60 states is attained; but those states' absence will certainly weaken the tribunal's claims to being representative of the World Community and also its political prestige and authority, more particularly as a considerable part of the new court's cases may be expected to arise from international armed conflicts in which those same states will be active participants or leaders.

The objections to the proposed new International Criminal Court were best articulated by U.S. spokespersons, and they focussed directly on the fear that U.S. political leaders and U.S. military personnel might, in the future, be subjected to prosecution before the court. These objections led directly to the unsuccessful attempt to insert in the Court Statute a requirement that prosecutions be required, first, to be approved by the U.N. Security Council, where, of course, the United States and also any of the other four Permanent Members of the Council would be able to exercise a legal right of Veto. But it was exactly the felt need that the proposed new court should be seen to be universal in its jurisdiction, without egregious exemptions in favour of any particular state or group of states, that clearly led the delegates to the U.N. Diplomatic Conference on the Establishment of an International Criminal Court, at the Rome session in July, 1998, that finally adopted the Court Statute, to put aside any thought of making any such special exceptions. The decision at Rome to opt for a strong court, as nearly as possible universal in its range and jurisdiction, with the risk of losing, thereby, some of the major powers as signatories and ratifiers, was thought preferable to having a lowest common denominator agreement with its text riddled with escape clauses as the inevitable price of rallying everyone to a "soft" drafting consensus. As a drafting exercise, the Court Statute represents a considerable advance in the progressive development of International Law on the principles considered and applied at the Nuremberg Tribunal in 1946. Article 5 of the Rome Statute establishes the four categories of international crimes within the jurisdiction of the court:

the crime of genocide; crimes against humanity; war crimes; and the crime of aggression.

The category of Crimes against Humanity was left to be defined concretely, an exercise for which U.N. General Assembly Resolution 3314 (XXIX) of 14 December 1974, itself the product of a marathon, interminable legal debate, provides a useful but only partial help.

Article 27 of the Statute (Irrelevance of official capacity) declares that official capacity as a Head of State or Government, a member of a Government or parliament, shall not exempt a person from criminal responsibility; and that legal immunities or special procedural rules attaching to the official capacity of a person, whether under national or international law, shall not bar court jurisdiction. Article 28 (Responsibility of commanders and other superiors), and Article 33 (Superior orders and prescription of Law), build on the Nuremberg principles by effectively establishing full responsibility for war crimes at the two levels, the ultimate military command and the soldiers actually carrying out the order. The detailed provisions on the Office of the Prosecutor, Article 42, insist on the independence of the prosecutor, and seem stronger than the practice of the *ad hoc* U.N. War Crimes tribunals on Yugoslavia and Rwanda in the express directive that the prosecutor and staff shall not seek or act on instructions from any external source.

The still ongoing U.N. experience with the *ad hoc* tribunals on Yugoslavia and Rwanda was undoubtedly studied by the delegates to the Rome diplomatic conference. Entry into force of the Rome Statute would presumably dispense with the need for any future such *ad hoc* tribunals, and in creating a permanent, full-time tribunal would also overcome some of the problems besetting the *ad hoc* tribunals. The *ad hoc* tribunals suffered from the fact that, being purely temporary in character, it was difficult to recruit and to retain long-term, internationally well-known or experienced international jurists as judges or supporting staff. This showed up, particularly, with the office of Prosecutor. The first two Prosecutors of the *ad hoc* tribunal on Yugoslavia left that office, in succession, in order to seek and accept appointments within their own national judicial systems. In the case of the second of the two Prosecutors, it meant leaving with only

54

half the term completed and after a well-publicised run for a judicial promotion at home that brought reminders of the U.S. Chief Prosecutor at Nuremberg in 1946, Robert Jackson (then on temporary leave from the U.S. Supreme Court) who had campaigned at long distance from Nuremberg for promotion to the office of the Chief Justice of the U.S. Supreme Court which suddenly became vacant during his term at Nuremberg. Both Prosecutors at the *ad hoc* Tribunal on Yugoslavia were criticised for spending time in travel on the international diplomatic circuit rather than on staying at the tribunal to work on the preparation of actual files, though this was no doubt explained by the early doubts as to the political viability of the office. In the second Prosecutor's case, there was also criticism for conferring, and being seen publicly to confer, with the U.S. Secretary of State and the British Foreign Secretary, this being argued by some to be inimical to the postulated independence of the office. But the *ad hoc* tribunals on Yugoslavia and Rwanda and the office of Prosecutor within the tribunals were *sui generis*; and they would have to develop their own precedents and practice. The new Prosecutor, named in August,1999, after the premature departure of the second incumbent of the office, was a national of Switzerland, not a member-state of the United Nations and not, of course, a member-state of the NATO military alliance. This would have an extra advantage of eliminating potential suggestions of being *parti pris* in any subsequent indictment of Yugoslavia political or military leaders and not at the same time of leaders of other states engaged in the conflict in post-Succession Yugoslavia.

There are many roads to Rome, in terms of the alternative legal arenas now available for pursuing alleged international crimes arising from the various armed conflicts in the years since the disintegration of Tito's Socialist Federal Republic of Yugoslavia began in 1989. On 3 June 1999, the International Court of Justice in The Hague, in 12-to-4 rulings (with the Russian and the Chinese judges among the Dissenters) declined to accept jurisdiction on separate legal complaints launched by the rump state of Yugoslavia against a number of the active combatant NATO member-states, that were based, *inter alia*, on the NATO forces' aerial bombardment of civilian populations and civil property within Yugoslavia.[16] However, the International Court of Justice's rulings were rendered on narrowly technical legal grounds, going to preliminary, jurisdictional questions only. They did not involve Court pronouncement on the substantive legal issues involved, which the Court and also individual judges in their Opinions were at some pains to leave open for possible future decision. As an interesting footnote, the U.S. Administration agreed, on 30 July 1999, to pay \$4.5 million (U.S. dollars) in respect to the Chinese citizens killed in the NATO forces' aerial bombardment of the Chinese Embassy in Belgrade during the course of the NATO states' armed action against Yugoslavia – an attack which NATO officials at the time characterised as an accident. In making the payment, the U.S. administration insisted that its diplomatic action was not an admission of legal liability by the U.S., thereby recalling the similar, though much delayed, action by the U.S. Administration in regard to the shooting down by U.S. armed forces of the Iranian unarmed, civil commercial passenger aircraft over the Persian Gulf, a decade earlier.[17]

Finally, if action should fail at the international level, in international legal arenas, for claimed redress against alleged breaches of International Law, the way may be open, on the legal example provided by British national courts in the case of ex-Chilean President, General Pinochet, for a successful legal process before municipal, national law courts, involving International Law norms as incorporated into national law either directly by legislation, or as part of the municipal common law *(jurisprudence)*. With the evident gaps in the effective jurisdiction of the new International Criminal Court, if and when its Statute should finally be ratified by the legally sufficient minimum number of States, individual or group processes before national courts and involving their own national laws may become the only way effectively to reach political and military leaders of those major powers that do not choose to ratify the Court Statute and thus hinder a more comprehensive and inclusive international application of the new International Criminal Law norms.

Chapter VI

INTERNATIONAL LAW-MAKING PROCESS
FOR A NEW WORLD ORDER:
THE WAR OF THE YUGOSLAV SUCCESSION

(a) The past as prologue: from Congress of Berlin, 1878, to the Versailles settlement, 1919

The continuing armed conflicts in the former Socialist Federal Republic of Yugoslavia extending throughout the last decade of the 20th century resemble very much those equally interminable and, in terms of the changing motivations of the various intervening States, the politically confused struggles in Europe at the opening and in the middle of the 18th century, known respectively as the Wars of the Spanish and the Austrian Succession. The ultimate historical roots of the internal armed conflicts of the 1990s in Marshal Tito's legacy of the state of Yugoslavia go back, as was widely noted in Western capitals at the time, more than six hundred years, to the Battle of Kosovo in 1389 when the mediaeval kingdom of Serbia fell to the new, expanding Ottoman Empire. More recent historical events, going back to the late 19th century, provide a more meaningful explanation of the confusions and rivalries of Western European states and their foreign ministries whose own national self-interests, as they defined them, were often on direct collision courses in South Eastern Europe and the Balkans and the Eastern Mediterranean. Imperial German and Austro-Hungarian *Drang nach Osten* foreign policy and trade imperatives collided with the Imperial Russian-inspired and encouraged Pan-Slavic movement and the Russian drive for warm-water "windows" on the Mediterranean. The waning Ottoman Empire – the "sick man of Europe" – was both the main problem and also the most obviously available means of solution for those rival Imperial expansionist drives. In Great Britain, there was an oscillation, in the late 19th century, between Gladstone Liberal and Disraeli Conservative foreign policy concepts. The British Liberals came close to the levels of end-of-20th century invective in "demonising" the opponent, with the demands for a form of humanitarian intervention to save alleged victims of religious oppression by what was

57

variously characterised as the "unspeakable Turk", the "abominable Turk". The British Conservatives, more prosaically and in line with classic British off-shore diplomacy towards Continental Europe, had attitudes rooted in balance-of-power considerations and in maintaining a strategic equilibrium between the main Continental European states. When the Russians, as the fruits of their successful military campaign in the Russo-Turkish War of 1877-8, proposed to carve up the Ottoman domains in the Balkans, in line with Russian Pan-Slavic preferences, through the Treaty of San Stefano in 1878, the Western European Concert of powers stepped in and, under masterful direction by Disraeli and Bismarck at the Congress of Berlin later in the same year, rewrote the map of the Balkans so as to accord with consensual, pan-European principles which respected, more adequately, the European political-military balance of power since the Congress of Vienna and the post-Napoleonic settlement of 1815. The Ottoman Empire was allowed to continue in South Eastern Europe and the Balkans, albeit in a territorially vastly reduced form, mainly because the Concert of European Ministers at the Congress of Berlin could think of nothing better to do with it that would succeed in maintaining the intra-European consensus. Serbia, Bulgaria and Romania emerged as independent mini-states, but within far more restricted territorial frontiers than ethno-cultural self-determination would otherwise have suggested. This was due in considerable measure not merely to Big-Power competitions over their own respective spheres of influence, but also, and more obviously, to the fact that noone in the Congress of Berlin was prepared, then, to give the time or the patience to sorting out and demarcating territorial boundaries for what were so often ethnically mixed and complex communities. Multi-cultural Bosnia-Herzegovina, because of its special geopolitical character as a region situated on the south-east boundary of the Austro-Hungarian Empire and on the direct expansionist route of the Imperial German *Drang nach Osten* trade and commercial drive, was handed over to the Austro-Hungarian Empire by the Berlin Congress under the polite euphemism of a Protectorate, with the legal formalities being finally dropped altogether, thirty years later, when it was incorporated into the Habsburg Empire.

The intra-European clashes within the Balkans, temporarily rationalised and halted by the Berlin Congress for the next three decades after 1878, had come out into the open again just before the outbreak of World War I. The two Balkan Wars of 1912-13, which had been planned and directed by the newly independent Balkan states as a means of finally expelling the Ottoman Empire from Europe, though yielding the first objective of the military defeat of Turkey, ended up in a form of Balkan civil war. As soon as Turkey had been disposed of militarily, members of the victorious alliance of new Balkan States began to feud among themselves over the division of the spoils, and the Big-Power sponsors of the contending, now rival Balkan States began to maneuver for their own political advantage, with consequences that carried over to the causes of the wider European war of 1914. The main losers after the Second Balkan War, Bulgaria and Turkey, were to join Germany and the Central Powers in World War I in the hope of recouping their failed territorial claims from the two Balkan Wars of 1912-13.

The final peace settlements to the great European War, 1914-1918, enshrined in the Treaty of Versailles and the related special treaties covering the territories of Austria-Hungary, Bulgaria, and the Ottoman Empire, if they had tried to render more than lip-service to U.S. President Woodrow Wilson's Fourteen Points, might have initiated a rational process of re-arrangement of territorial frontiers within the Balkans so as to reduce the risk of future conflicts by respecting more determinedly the principle of self-determination of peoples along ethno-cultural lines. This was never seriously attempted, however, and perhaps it could not have been attempted, even if the original intent had been there, granted the obvious imperfections as to knowledge and expertise on the Balkans on the part of the Western European Big Three at Versailles in 1919 – Clemenceau, Lloyd George, and Orlando – and their specialist advisers. The largest considerations for the victorious Western European leaders at Versailles, once they had moved on from their announced primary concerns of determination of War guilt, of imposition of reparations on defeated Germany, and of disposition of the German colonies in Africa and the South Pacific, to putatively secondary issues of Eastern and South-Eastern Europe and the Middle East, were a continuation of the "spoils to the victors" politic that they had already sought to apply in the main Versailles Treaty itself. The Western European Big Three's Carthaginian approach dictated severe territorial sanctions against Hungary (now split off from Austria, with the dissolution of the old Habsburg Empire), and Bulgaria, and the Ottoman Empire, and also corresponding expansion of the victorious Western European coalition's lesser allies in those regions. The Classical, measured European balance-of-power approach – a peace settlement without victors and vanquished, such as diplomatically brokered in Vienna in 1815 – was put aside in favour of a custodial peace in a Europe whose security would be ensured, less by Woodrow Wilson's ideal of the new League of Nations, than by an interlocking system of Continental regional military alliances. These post-Versailles military alliances would be based upon the new succession states to the old Empires of Austria-Hungary and Russia, and also upon territorially-inflated, already existing states like Romania and like Serbia (now, after 1919, the Kingdom of the Serbs, Croats, and Slovenes).

The territorial aggrandisement of the new, or newly remade Succession states under the Versailles and related peace treaties was not always desired or pursued by those states themselves. Their leaders, from their own direct historical experience, were often more aware than the Western European leaders and diplomats gathered at Versailles of the immense practical difficulties involved in containing unwilling minorities within fragile multinational states that were inexperienced in the skills of pragmatism and compromise needed to construct and then to hold together federal or similar plural-constitutional governmental systems. Some of the Serbian leaders at Versailles are known to have preferred a territorially somewhat more modest and certainly ethno-culturally far more homogeneous "Greater Serbia," that would group together Serbian religious and cultural communities that had had common historical experience in the fight against Ottoman rule, and that amounted to majority or near-majority numbers in different areas. Instead, the larger and much looser multi-national kingdom that the Western European leaders eventually imposed would have to bridge not merely the two different religions and religious structures, Roman Catholic and Serbian Orthodox, but also to transcend the great historical fault line, going back for some centuries now, between constituent units like Slovenia and Croatia that had been under Austrian and Hungarian rule respectively and that had thereby been oriented to the West in a political-cultural sense, and Serbia-Montenegro whose historical heritage had been distant conquest and then many centuries of subjection to the Islamic Ottoman rule.

The decision, instead of a territorially more limited and homogeneous Greater Serbia which might have been rounded off, peacefully, through the processes of public consultation and vote and subsequent voluntary transfer and exchange of populations of the sort that had been perfected, under League of Nations' auspices, for German and Polish minorities conflicts-resolutions in the 1920s, to opt for the larger, multi-cultural Kingdom of the Serbs, Croats, and Slovenes, seems to have come from two rather different considerations. Under the secret agreement and undertakings made to Italy by the Western European allies, in 1916, to induce Italy to leave its long-standing military alliance with the Central Powers and to join the West, territorial satisfaction had been promised to Italy from the Adriatic coast domains of the Austro-Hungarian Empire. For Slovenian and Croatian political leaders in the corridors at Versailles in 1919, joining the new Serb-Croat-Slovene state may have seemed a better gamble, politically, than being absorbed into Italy. Another, countervailing consideration was the Realpolitik argument that while a strong Yugoslavia would be a necessary political instrument for preserving the Western European-imposed, Versailles and related peace treaties' settlements in the Balkans, the new Yugoslavia should not be allowed to become so strong as to upset or threaten the European balance-of-power outside the Balkans region itself. A multi-national state with the continuing inner tensions that that would involve in a Balkan context would be an effective political check-and-balance against any Serbian ambitions to overweening power in the Balkans.

The history of the new Kingdom of the Serbs, Croats, and Slovenes, after 1919, confirmed the accuracy of the advance predictions of the problems in uniting, within one state, disparate acquired cultures stemming from radically different exposures to foreign governments, even when one community in strictly ethnic terms was involved. Yugoslavia, between the two World Wars, was transformed into a highly centralised unitary state governed from Belgrade. Recurrent breakaway, terrorist activity culminating in the assassination, apparently with support from Mussolini's Italian Government, of the King of Yugoslavia and the French Foreign Minister in 1934, led on in World War II to German and Italian and Bulgarian military occupations of Yugoslavia. This followed on the German *Luftwaffe's* aerial bombardment of Belgrade in 1941, immediately prior to the German invasion of Russia. In political-territorial terms, it meant the creation of a German-sponsored state of Croatia, as well as vastly expanded new territories for Albania and Bulgaria, all at the expense of Yugoslavia. The Yalta Agreement between the Big Three Allied leaders, in February, 1945, paved the way to restoration of Yugoslavia in its original, pre-1941 frontiers, and led on to Tito's successive experiments in territorial devolution of power within the framework of his Communist Party-led, Socialist Federal Republic of Yugoslavia. It was widely forecast that Tito's federation would not long survive his own demise. This proved to be an accurate historical prediction, though the actual dissolution or disintegration of the Tito federation would not take place until after the fall of the Berlin Wall in 1989 and the symbolic ending of the Cold War and of the comfortably secure and politically predictable Bipolar system of world public order that had been developed and consolidated throughout the long period of East-West *détente*.

(b) International Recognition of State Succession in Yugoslavia

The emergence of a new state, whether by merger of existing states or by dissolution or breakaway in the case of an existing state, occurs under International Law today at two different levels. First, entry into the international community is determined by the action of other states which choose, under their own municipal, national law to recognise a claimed new state entity. Second, entry into the United Nations is determined according to the Charter of the United Nations and encompasses the two different categories. These are, first, under Article 3 of the U.N. Charter, original members, meaning those present at the creation of the United Nations in San Francisco in the Spring of 1945 and thus limited effectively to states that had joined the ultimately victorious World War II military alliance; and second, under Article 4(1) and(2) of the Charter, "peace-loving states which accept the obligations contained in the ... Charter and ... are able and willing to carry out those obligations", but which are also admitted by a special constitutional process requiring an affirmative decision of the General Assembly upon the recommendation of the Security Council (to which latter, as a deemed "important" matter, the Veto of any of the five Permanent Members of the Security Council would apply),

Both status conditions – recognition by other states, and admission to the United Nations, have acquired their own corpus of developed legal practice and rules. Recognition, though exercised by each state individually, is governed and limited by larger principles of International Law subsumed under two different theories, the Constitutive theory of Recognition and the Declaratory theory. The Constitutive theory developed in Classical International law under the influence of neo-Kantian liberal thinking and was posited upon the free will of the state actors involved to accept or not to accept a claimed new state as a member of the international community and endowed, as such, with the full attributes of legal sovereignty. The recognition by any one state would be legally controlling as to its own municipal, national law; and the recognition by a sufficiency of other states would be legally constitutive in terms of creating a new International Law fact.

In contrast, under the Declaratory theory of recognition, a recognising state would be simply moving to accord its own municipal, national law with the objective facts of the international community and with whether or not a claimed new entity had in fact come into being as a political fact.

As examples of the Constitutive theory of recognition in its negative implication we have the long-sustained historical non-Recognition by

Western states of non-Christian states like Turkey, and of non-European states like China and Japan. Judge and later President of the International Court of Justice, Mohammed Bedjaoui, appearing before the Court in an earlier capacity as legal counsel in the *Western Sahara* Advisory Opinion,[1] identified three successive epochs in the evolution of the Constitutive theory: Roman antiquity, when any territory not occupied by Romans was considered as *terra nullius*; the epoch of the great European discoveries of the 16th and 17th centuries during which any territory, not belonging to a Christian sovereign was also considered *terra nullius*; and finally the 19th century, when any territory not belonging to a deemed "civilised" state was presumed to be in the same category.

The doctrine of recognition, by the end of the 19th century and the early 20th century, had begun to move from voluntarist to objectivist criteria for rationalising and justifying state decisions on recognition and non-recognition. The development of international trade and commerce, in keeping with liberal market economy ideas, had brought a new emphasis on a claimed new state or government's international credit standing and its ability and willingness to honour its foreign loans and to repay external debts, and also to maintain the letter or spirit of contracts and concessions extended to foreign creditor states. This shift from voluntarist to objectivist criteria brought forward, logically enough, new concepts of a *duty* of recognition, where a new state or government demonstrably had accepted and fulfilled the accepted "rules of the game" of the World trading community. Not surprisingly, it was Great Britain which led the way, as the most powerful World trading community pre-1914, with the Pound Sterling serving as international currency and the British Navy enforcing its will where needed.

Within the contours of the objectivist *doctrines* on recognition and the postulated duty of recognition of new states and governments in order to bring one's own law into line with new political facts of international society, various sub-*doctrines* emerged, including a duty of non-Recognition. This latter implied a correlative duty to avoid "premature" recognition before an emerging new state or government should establish itself effectively; and before, certainly, the position of an original parent state or government, from which a new political movement or authority was seeking to break away, should have become hopeless and beyond political or military redemption. The *doctrinal*-legal principle on the legal duty of non-Recognition (the legal duty to avoid *premature* recognition, at least) had been developed and refined in the special context of the Spanish Civil War in the late 1930s, where the British and French Governments' brokering of the Non-Intervention Agreement and also decisions by their municipal, national courts, were criticised by legal publicists as amounting to a *de facto* recognition of the rebel, Franco forces in Spain, at a time when the Spanish Civil War was still in full fury and when the original, democratically-elected Republican Government of Spain was still in effective political and military control of the national capital and also of a large part of the national territory.

The decision by the German Government, in December, 1991, to recognise then constituent units of the Socialist Federal Republic of Yugoslavia, has been criticised on International Law grounds as an example of a "premature" recognition of breakaway states of an existing international legal person still in effective control of its own legal territories. The breakaway entities concerned were Slovenia, Croatia, and Bosnia-Herzegovina. The German Government decision has also been criticised on political grounds as creating, – before appropriate control structures and processes had been devised and put in place to fill the resultant political vacuum – a "falling dominoes" effect, leading on to the other attempted breakaways from Yugoslavia such as FYROM (the United Nations temporary characterisation of Slavic-Macedonia) and eventually Kosovo, and also precipitating the cruel, internecine conflict in Bosnia-Herzegovina. The German Foreign Ministry also spearheaded the political pressures within the United Nations in1992 in behalf of the speedy admission to the United Nations of the same three breakaway states from Yugoslavia – Slovenia, Croatia, and Bosnia-Herzegovina.

These German diplomatic initiatives in behalf of Slovenia and Croatia at least, strongly supported as they were by other Western European states and the United States, could be justified on their own special sociological facts. Both new states, because of their past long-time status as parts of the Austro-Hungarian Empire, fell on the Western side of the historical East-West civilisation fault-line cutting through the centre of Yugoslavia as established by the victors at Versailles, in 1919. They had certainly been a principal preoccupation of the German Foreign Ministry in the German-French rivalry in the Balkans up to 1914 which seemed, somewhat anachronistically, to be repeating itself in the early 1990s. Bosnia-Herzegovina, in contrast, would fit in somewhat strangely with the other two Yugoslav Succession states, for its links with Austria-Hungary commenced only as late as 1878 with the "protectorate" conferred by the Congress of Berlin in that year. The Protectorate was later to be converted to direct annexation by the Austro-Hungarian Empire in 1908. But it had all been ended, once and for all, with the Versailles and related Peace treaties of 1919.

The most valid criticism of the "premature" recognitions of 1992 would go, not to the substantive grounds for the ultimate decision but to the failure to act with any large, comprehensive vision of the consequences of one's act, or with a rational over-all plan and vision for the future of the Balkan region as a whole if the dissolution of Tito's Socialist Federal Republic was to be taken as the eventual desideratum. The political leaders at the Congress of Berlin in 1878 had just such a larger vision and their settlement lasted for forty years until overwhelmed by World War I. There was, as already noted, no Bismarck or Disraeli in the key Western European governments at the time of the effective dissolution of Yugoslavia in 1991-2. The result was purely *ad hoc* diplomatic remedies taken out of any larger strategic context and seemingly involving the reopening of the old Foreign Ministry dossiers from pre-1914. The particular sectorial accord, among the Versailles peace treaties of 1919, that had created the Kingdom of the Serbs, Croats and Slovenes, the Treaty of St. Germain-en-Laye, contained its own in-built machinery and processes for revision or modification of the provisions of the treaty, if they should be found to be wanting. These included reference at a certain stage to the Compulsory Jurisdiction of the Permanent Court of International Justice (now International Court of Justice), and this at the instance, unilaterally, of any one of the State signatories to the treaty.[2]

In retrospect, another Congress of Berlin-style Concert of the European powers, convened in 1990 or 1991, before the internal situation in the Socialist Federal Republic of Yugoslavia had become pathological and politically out-of-hand, might have helped avert or at least moderate the subsequent extended armed conflicts. It need not have delayed or avoided recognition of Slovenia and Croatia or their admission to the United Nations. But those acts might simply have been predicated upon reaching agreement on a process for peaceful adjustment of the existing, internal boundaries of the Socialist Federal Republic of Yugoslavia's constituent federal republics to contemporary ethno-cultural facts; and, if rectification of those internal frontiers should not be found to be politically practicable, then for peaceful voluntary exchanges or transfers of civil populations on the basis of the effective control of Germany-Poland minorities problems operated under the League of Nations auspices in the 1920s.

(c) International (Regional) Armed Intervention
against Yugoslavia

The end of the 20th century and the approach of the new millennium have
provided the occasion for historical review and for attempting some sort of
balance sheet of human achievement and failure during the past century.
Political leaders will do well to remember the philosopher, Santayana's
maxim that those who don't study history are condemned to repeat its
errors. Some of the more interesting contemporary historical analysis of
the century just passing has been directed to the events at the opening of
the century, with the delayed ending, in 1914, of the 19th century and of
the Congress of Vienna-brokered, century of relative peace and security
among the leading World powers of the day. This century of Peace had
resulted from the highly pragmatic, pan-European consensus at the
Congress of Vienna in 1815, which came at the end of a generation of massive armed conflict. There is, by now, sufficient intellectual detachment, in
space and time, from the events of the War of 1914-18, for professional
historians to be able to disengage themselves from the officially organised
propaganda and "demonisation" of the opposing side practised by both of
the rival military alliances of the time. This has meant, at long last, no
longer placing War guilt totally on the vanquished enemy states of 1914-
18; and it has also meant trying to reach a politically balanced final judgment, with the conclusion that it was a failure of diplomacy and of rational judgment on the part of political leaders that produced what is now
described, variously, as an unnecessary war, a "European civil war" –

> "something worse than a tragedy, which we are taught by the theatre to
> regard as ultimately unavoidable. It was nothing less than the greatest
> error of modern history." [3]

British Prime Minister Lloyd George, a highly pragmatic politician who
was intelligent enough personally to reject any "evil man" view of history
and the conclusion from that that it was the German Kaiser who had per-
fidiously planned the First World War, thought that it was, rather, something into which the European political leaders of the day had staggered
and stumbled, having neither the intellectual energy nor the imagination to
stem and control the march of events from the assassinations at Sarajevo
on June 28, 1914, on through the next five weeks up to the actual outbreak
of armed hostilities. Kurt Joos, in his ballet "The Green Table", launched
at the opening of the 1930s when the forces that would produce the next
World War were already at work, rendered the events pictorially as a group

66

of elderly statesmen attired in prime diplomatic regalia, playing a futile dance of musical chairs around a classical negotiating table.

Part of the problem at the close of the 20th century has been a constant changing of the guard, politically, in most of the major powers. The generation of political and military leaders who went through the fires of World War II had passed from the World political scene by the opening of the 1990s. The U.S. President at century's end, President Clinton, was the first U.S. President since War's end in 1945 without direct personal military experience in war or even in peace. He had not himself served in the Vietnam War, and his homologues in the main Western European countries – in Great Britain and Germany as notable examples – had all been "peace activists" in 1968, campaigning as students in their own, then neutral countries against the U.S. engagement in the war in Vietnam. The remarkable achievement of NATO, in its original, Cold War historical role as a Western defensive alliance against the Soviet Union-directed Warsaw Pact military alliance had been that its political and military leaders, with their own direct, active combat experience, tried, for the most part successfully, to avoid using war as an instrument of collective policy; and where armed action occurred or appeared to threaten, they used their best skills to put an end to the international tensions by non-military means. With the Korean War – a conflict that, in historical retrospect, may perhaps now be judged to be one into which the opposing sides staggered or stumbled on the World War I model, the best intelligence was employed to contain its operation as a more limited "regional" conflict and to prevent it from escalating into a full East-West confrontation (the Truman phase); and then to negotiate a conclusion on an inter-bloc, mutual give-and-take basis (the Eisenhower phase). The striking feature of the history of the Cold War, thereafter, was the development of effective techniques and processes of inter-bloc crisis management and conflicts-resolution, with measured escalation to any military action, (as in the Kennedy-Khrushchev peaceful resolution of the Cuban Missile crisis in 1962), and, in the end, without any actual recourse to the use of armed force. It was, of course, a conservative, political status quo-oriented, approach to inter-bloc relations; and the price to pay, on the Western side, was some certain sacrifice of professed concern for Western "Open Society" values, including therein the principle of self-determination of peoples, as in the Czechoslovakian crisis of 1968 when the Western powers accepted, out of felt necessity, the territorial integrity of Soviet bloc frontiers as defined and legitimated in the Yalta and Potsdam accords.

The key questions in regard to the U.S. decision to intervene militarily, with direct application of armed force, against Yugoslavia in the Kosovo situation in March, 1999, must be, *first*, why at that particular time; and then, whether all the alternative, more moderate controls not involving recourse to armed force, had first been tried and exhausted before the final decision to move was taken. The *second* question must be why the particular vehicle for application of armed force, NATO, was chosen, rather than opting to proceed, on the basis of all existing contemporary precedents, through the United Nations. This approach would have involved securing the necessary International Law base, through U.N. Security Council or General Assembly Resolutions, to create a multi-national U.N. armed force operating under U.N. aegis and command (as in the Korean crisis of 1950); or else proceeding, under the umbrella legal authority of a series of enabling Security Council Resolutions, to endow a multi-state alliance led by the U.S. with plenary legal powers to go ahead (as in the Gulf War crisis of 1990-1).

There have been suggestions that the actual recourse to armed force was premature, before the other options had been fully explored, and that the Rambouillet Accord (the Interim Agreement for Peace and Self-Government in Kosovo) of February 23, 1999, was intentionally framed as a form of ultimatum inviting rejection on the part of the Yugoslav Government. The principal state actors at Rambouillet had all been involved in the earlier impasse over Bosnia-Herzegovina, (though in the case of some of those states with different governments); and all had been subject to the criticism of having reacted too tardily and too weakly to prevent the tragic loss of civilian lives among all of the parties to that earlier conflict. The U.N. Secretary-General of that earlier period when the ultimate political-territorial disposition of Bosnia-Herzegovenia was the key item on the international agenda, has, in his recent memoirs, identified the then U.S. Ambassador to the United Nations and subsequent Secretary of State during the Kosovo crisis as having earlier argued for the use of air strikes to resolve the Bosnian crisis and as having then blamed the United Nations for their failure.[4] The fact remains that the Rambouillet accords, if accepted, would have amounted to a far more drastic surrender of Yugoslav state sovereignty than the ultimate cease-fire agreement that was drafted by the G-8 countries and accepted by Yugoslavia only after the NATO eleven-week aerial bombardment, and that was embodied in U.N. Security Council Resolution 1244 (1999), adopted on 10 June 1999. That cease-fire agreement accepts, in terms, a continuing Yugoslav authority predicated upon a "substantial autonomy" for the people of Kosovo "within the Federal Republic of Yugoslavia." The difference between the Rambouillet accords and the subsequent, U.N. Security Council-approved settlement was undoubtedly a consequence of the difference in their timing, from February to June of 1999, and the unsettling effect of the unforeseen, unexpectedly long, eleven-week aerial bombardment that was eventually required to bring Yugoslavia back to a negotiated agreement. It also reflected the diplomatic conclusion on the part of the Western and Western European military intervenors that a substantial Russian involvement was necessary before the Yugoslav Government would come to terms, and that this involved some amelioration, at least, of the original hard-line Western and Western European approach. The only other realistic option open for the military intervenors would have involved their switching over to an ever more intensive and comprehensive form of military engagement, involving the commitment of ground forces. But this had already been judged as unacceptable to public opinion in the military intervenor states, whose continuing involvement in the alliance was predicated in considerable measure on the original public promise of a no-risk, high-tech war, with the guarantee of "no-casualties" on the part of the military intervenor states themselves.

Why NATO, with the conscious by-passing of the United Nations and its highly-developed peace-keeping and peace-making machinery that that particular choice involved? One clear answer, certainly, would be a certain impatience, on the U.S. side, with the United Nations and the extended legal procedures involved in its collective decision-making which were blamed for the delays and indecisiveness and, in the end, the limited effectiveness of the U.N. peace-making in Bosnia-Herzegovina. Again, however er the extended history of that Bosnia-Herzegovina operation given by the U.N. Secretary-General of the time, Boutros Boutros-Ghali,[5] would suggest that the failures in Bosnia-Herzegovina may have had more to do with the gaps in the diplomatic problem-solving skills of the key Western state actors than with the United Nations! The NATO leadership, the civilian and also the military commanders, may also bear some responsibility for the resultant problems. In responding too eagerly to the opportunity for a continued political-military *rôle*, post-Cold War, they may have failed adequately to warn the Western political leaders calling on them to intervene in Yugoslavia both of the doubts as to NATO's legal power to act in the absence of a prior enabling authority from the U.N. Security Council or General Assembly, and also of the technical-logistical limitations on NATO's capacity to deliver the desired military result within the desired short time-frame, granted the fact that NATO's special professional military competence had been developed and exercised for the quite different purpose of preserving peace and a nuclear balance-of-power between the two great political-military blocs during the Cold War. Nothing in NATO's forty years of highly successful operation as a Cold War defensive military alliance directed against the former Soviet Union and its allies had prepared its civilian or military command for the sophisticated, mixed political-military and sometimes outright political decisions required for the Balkans and for dealing with the former Socialist Federal state of Yugoslavia and its various successor-states. Yugoslavia itself had withdrawn very early from the Soviet bloc military alliance system after Marshal Tito's break with Stalin and his opting, first, for "Deviationism" within the Soviet bloc and thereafter for a politic of deliberate Non-Alignment in the continuing East-West Cold War conflicts.

Some explanations for the U.S. Administration's opting for a hard-line, no-compromise approach to the government of rump Yugoslavia in early 1999 after its earlier, at least tacit, cooperation with Belgrade in the run-up to a solution of the Bosnia-Herzegovina conflict and to the resulting Dayton, Ohio, accords, have sought political links to the crisis in U.S. internal politics in early 1999 which produced the near-miss of the constitutional Impeachment process launched by the U.S. Congress against President Clinton. The sudden switch, in a matter of a few months only, from the U.S. Central Intelligence Agency's original classification of the Albanian-directed Kosovo Liberation Army as an international terrorist organisation, to the acceptance of the K.L.A. by the U.S. Administration as some sort of popular liberation force, might appear to lend credence to just such an interpretation. However, the better view would appear to be that the decision to opt for NATO-based armed action against Yugoslavia stemmed from a conjunction of the U.S. long-range political disaffection and impatience with the United Nations as a collective decision-making body for the World Community, and of a seriously flawed estimate of NATO's inherent capacities for analysing complex problem-situations in the Balkans region and for producing timely and practical military and political-military solutions for them.

For individual member-states of NATO that had been the long-time allies of NATO's leader, the United States, the sudden call to arms against rump Yugoslavia by the U.S. President demanded an immediate response without effective time for raising military-logistical doubts or for pressing for explanation as to the non-recourse to alternative, more moderate controls not involving direct use of armed force. It was not perhaps an appropriate occasion for questioning the *raison d'être* of NATO and its continued practical utility in the post-Cold War era, though that sort of critical questioning and cost-benefit analysis would very likely be forthcoming after the military operation should have ended. In the meantime, those of the NATO states that responded to the U.S. President's call and agreed, some for the first time, to cross the line from U.N. peace-*keeping* (Chapter VI of the U.N. Charter) to U.N. peace-*making* (Chapter VII of the Charter) put efforts forward, with varying degrees of energy and enthusiasm, both to widen the group of participants in order to go beyond the closed group of NATO member-states, and also to bring the whole action under the legal authority, if not yet the effective political and military direction and control, of the United Nations. Both initiatives were eventually successful, helped by the demonstrable fact, as the NATO high-level bombing campaign extended well beyond the original forecast of a one week campaign to eleven weeks, that the alternative might have to be an even more prolonged war involving commitment of ground forces and, inevitably, failure of the original "no casualties" objective for the military intervenor states' armed forces. A direct involvement of Russia in the approach to a political solution had been one of the proposals first advanced by Greek Prime Minister Simitis who also had the idea of giving a pan-Balkan flavour to the pursuit of peaceful solutions through enlisting the Balkan neighbour states of Yugoslavia. Greece and Italy had both been very effective, as "good neighbours" entering at the invitation of the Albanian President a year earlier, in ending near civil war, internal strife in Albania.

Bringing Russia into the decision-making processes was the eventual key to ending the armed conflict over Kosovo. The vehicle for this was a G-8 Summit meeting, Russia, of course, being part of the G-8 group. The G-8-brokered solution gave Yugoslavia somewhat more than the Rambouillet accords, presented on a take-it-or-leave-it basis, had offered. It also allowed the NATO political and military command to cease their unexpectedly difficult aerial bombardment operation without loss of political face. Henceforth, the G-8 processes would displace NATO councils as the effective political decision-making arena. The formal declaration issued by the Chairman of the G-8 Foreign Ministers after their meeting on the Petersberg, Germany, on 6 May 1999, invokes, repeatedly, the United Nations, with references, variously, to "effective international civil and security presences in Kosovo endorsed and adopted by the United Nations", and to the "establishing of an interim administration for Kosovo to be decided by the Security Council of the United Nations". The Petersberg declaration concludes with an instruction by the G-8 Foreign Ministers to "prepare elements of a United Nations Security Council resolution". The declaration by the G-8 Foreign Ministers makes a point of stating that the G-8 Presidency will inform the Chinese government on the results of the meeting. There is no mention at all, however, of NATO.

U.N. Security Council Resolution 1244 (1999), adopted on 10 June 1999, which effectively signalled a legal end to the armed conflict by NATO forces with Yugoslavia, refers in terms in its Preambles to the Petersberg declaration made by the G-8 Ministers on 6 May 1999. It also includes the Petersberg declaration's statement of general principles for a political solution to the Kosovo crisis, as an annexure to the Resolution. (Annex 1: Statement by the Chairman on the conclusion of the meeting of the G-8 Foreign Ministers held at the Petersberg Centre on 6 May 1999).

(d) The United Nations and Contemporary International Law: the Kosovo action as case study

The Kosovo action and its final solution have some clear lessons to offer as to the contemporary International law-making process. In a widely quoted address to the American Society of International Law in Washington, D.C., in the spring of 1963, Dean Acheson who, as U.S. Secretary of State during the Korean War crisis of 1950 had presided over the evolution of the Uniting-for-Peace doctrine of plenary legal powers for the U.N. General Assembly if the Security Council should become blocked by the Big Power Veto in the exercise of its primary responsibility for maintenance of international peace and security, offered a *Staatsraison* defence for the "quarantine" measures applied by a later President, John Kennedy and a later Secretary of State, Dean Rusk, to resolve the October, 1962 Cuban Missile crisis. In Dean Acheson's words:

> "I must conclude that the propriety of the Cuban quarantine is not a legal issue. The power, position and prestige of the United States had been challenged by another state: and law simply does not deal with questions of ultimate power − power that comes close to the sources of sovereignty ... The survival of states is not a matter of law."[6]

The most challenging response to this, perhaps, is the comment by the Principal Legal Adviser to the State Department during the Cuban Missile crisis, Professor Abe Chayes of the Harvard Law School, who had been present throughout President Kennedy's discussion and planning for resolution of the Cuban Missile crisis:

> "The confrontation was not in the courtroom and in a world destructible by man, a legal position was obviously not the sole ingredient of effec-

tive action. We were armed, necessarily, with something more substantial than a lawyer's brief. But though it would not have been enough merely to have the law on our side, it is not irrelevant which side the law was on. The effective deployment of force, the appeal for world support, to say nothing of the ultimate judgment of history, all depend in significant degree on the reality and coherence of the case in law for our action."[7]

The *first* lesson from the Kosovo action is to bring the Legal Adviser in, from the beginning, to the crisis planning; and then to make to sure that legal counsel is heard, at the critical times when the choice between alternative means of crisis solution is being weighed, as to which options can be exercised compatibly with International Law and which cannot. The Legal Advisers do not seem to have been too very much involved when the macro-policies as to Kosovo, involving recourse to direct military action and application of armed force, were being considered and adopted. Even more, with the decisions on high-level aerial bombardment, while legal counsel was apparently available in NATO operational centres on day-by-day target bombing, legal advice does not seem to have been sought on the larger issues of how and why the ground rules as to aerial bombardment might have been changed by the more recent, post-World War II, legislative codifications of the law as to air warfare and its application to civilian targets.

The *second* lesson from the Kosovo action must be a reaffirmation of the primacy of the United Nations and its principal organs – the Security Council, the General Assembly, and the International Court of Justice – in international law-making and , in particular, as the only international institutions having the legal capacity to offer a legal exemption or dispensation from the United Nations Charter's legal outlawing of the use-of-force. The Kosovo military action and the recourse to armed force against rump Yugoslavia began wholly outside the United Nations, but ended up, appropriately enough, in the United Nations with United Nations Security Council Resolution 1244 (1999) of 10 June 1999. The U.N. Security Council Resolution finally closed the circle in International Law terms. In view of the fears expressed of a potential Russian or Chinese Veto if the proposed collective military action on Kosovo had first been submitted to the Security Council, it is worth recording that the Security Council vote that ended the collective military action was adopted with the affirmative vote of the Russian member of the Council, and with the Chinese member simply abstaining.

The *third* lesson is that the Law of War as to aerial bombardment, which could have been up-dated at Nuremberg in 1946 but was not in fact addressed in that tribunal's judgment, and which was more recently considered, and partly codified, in the 1977 Protocols Additional to the Geneva Conventions of 1949, calls out for new doctrinal study, in depth, and perhaps for a comprehensive international codification. Such a mandate might be given to a specialist commission of the *Institut de Droit International* or of the London-based International Law Association, or to the United Nations' own International Law Commission, or even to a special law-making conference appointed by the United Nations General Assembly. In any case, the further issue of the applicability of the new 1977 rules to non-signatories or non-ratifiers of the Protocols Additional to the Geneva Conventions of 1949, needs to be addressed. An Advisory Opinion reference by the United Nations to the International Court of Justice would, of course, provide the opportunity for a definitive, authoritative legal ruling.

The *fourth* lesson is that the claimed new International Law of Humanitarian Intervention, in spite of any legal errors and miscalculations in its invocation in aid of the Kosovo armed action, continues in progressive development in accordance with the U.N. Charter. The U.N. Security Council, in its Resolution 1244 (1999) of 10 June 1999, certainly did not, in any direct way, approve or ratify the NATO action; but neither did the Security Council take an obvious, ready-made opportunity for condemning the NATO action. In the religious philosopher, Reinhold Niebuhr's words, truth may sometimes ride into history on the back of an error. The next time, however, any international venture in exercise of a claimed right of Humanitarian Intervention should sensibly come only with the full legal authority and political weight of a prior, enabling Resolution of the U.N. Security Council or General Assembly directed, in terms, to the specific problem-situation involved. The legal issues as to a right of Humanitarian Intervention might all have been addressed, in ample time, in the long-political lead-up to the Kosovo action. They were in fact adverted to in the debates in the Canadian House of Commons as early as October, 1998, when the nature of the then styled, "inchoate" international legal claim to Humanitarian Intervention, was raised and canvassed.[8]

The *fifth* lesson must be one of the more useful ones learnt from the Cold War experience of crisis management, and that goes to the merits of lowering the rhetorical content of the debate and of avoiding ideological name-calling. Too much talk of a "Just War" in the abstract, without then getting into concrete details of the precise consequences of its invocation and then its practical application, impedes the search for rational solutions not involving unnecessary escalation to the use of armed force. The meeting of heads of government in Sarajevo on 30 July 1999, in pursuit of what was styled as a Stability Pact for Southeastern Europe, designed, as it was announced, to promote democracy and economic prosperity in the Balkans in the aftermath of the armed intervention against Kosovo, would appear headed for failure, after all the history of the victorious allies' treatment of the losing states in World War I and World War II, if it is intended to be confined to one or more states only, at the expense of a far more comprehensive and inclusive, regional, pan-Balkan approach. Stigmatising any one state and its population and trying to punish it by excluding it altogether from the post-war economic and social reconstruction of the whole region, would be to have learnt nothing and forgotten nothing as to the long-range dangers inherent in the political vacuum created by the wartime victors in central Europe in 1919 and again in 1945. Not merely the Kosovo sector but also all the neighbouring states to Yugoslavia in the Balkans suffered severely from the NATO states' armed intervention – among other things from the forced interruption, through NATO aerial bombardment of the Danube bridges, of the free flow of civil, trade, and commercial traffic on a river that had been effectively internationalised, under International Law, for well over a century. Financial compensation by NATO to the riparian states for such damage, and also NATO's participation in its rapid correction, would seem to be a clear and immediate obligation flowing from the armed intervention.

The *sixth* lesson, in deference to the legal principle that justice must not only be done but also be seen to be done, is that current War crimes processes in relation to the former Socialist Federal Republic of Yugoslavia and its various successor states may, for the future, sensibly have to be distanced from the NATO member-states that participated in the armed intervention in Kosovo in the Spring of 1999[9]. Such a policy may already have been initiated by U.N. Secretary-General Kofi Annan, with his selection of a jurist from neutral Switzerland as the new chief prosecutor for the *ad hoc* Tribunal for War Crimes in Yugoslavia where the opportunity presented itself, fortuitously, with the early resignation of the incumbent. Ideally, if and when the International Criminal Court whose Treaty was signed in Rome in July, 1998, should finally come into full legal force and operation, the *ad hoc* Tribunal for Yugoslavia might be absorbed or assimilated in to it. The extent of the commitment of states, including states that are Permanent Members of the Security Council to the principle of punishment of War Crimes and Crimes against Humanity, wherever they may be committed, may be tested operationally by those states' own ratification of the Rome Treaty without undue dragging of feet or without crippling reservations.

(e) Epilogue to Kosovo: United Nations action in East Timor

That the lessons to be drawn from the NATO armed intervention in Kosovo as to the *how, when,* and *why* of asserting a new International Law-based right of Humanitarian Intervention are now beginning to be understood and, more importantly, to be applied, may perhaps be seen in the World Community collective response to the East-Timor post-referendum crisis in mid-September, 1999. There were, to be sure, special military-logistical factors that might help explain the difference between the Kosovo and East Timor actions. East Timor was far away from the U.S. and Western Europe and from the effective range and reach of their operational military forces. Further, NATO's mandate for an armed intervention without any prior United Nations authorising Resolution, severely stretched as it may have been in the case of Kosovo, would have had to be pushed to extreme limits to justify any such collective action in East Timor. And Huntington's thesis as to the civilisation fault-lines, which had some passing relevance at least to the Kosovo conflict in so far as the identified line of divide between Western and Eastern Europe passed right through the centre of the Balkan region, would have become paramount with any U.S. and Western military operation launched in an Asian geopolitical context. There was no hesitation, in the World Community response to the East Timor post-referendum crisis, in going immediately to the U.N. Security Council for legal authority to intervene through an international military force operating under the aegis of the United Nations, and legally and militarily responsible to the United Nations, and endowed by the United Nations with U.N. Charter Chapter VII (peace-*making*) powers in addition to the more usual Chapter VI (peace-*keeping*) powers. Nobody raised, in advance of the U.N. Security Council vote on 15 September 1999, the menace of a possible Russian or Chinese Veto in the Security Council. No such Russian or Chinese Veto was in fact applied in the Security Council. The U.N. Security Council Resolution[10] was adopted by unanimous vote, including the concurring votes of all the Permanent Members.

NOTES TO THE FOREWORD

1. "The United Nations' recognition of new states and state succession",in *International Law at the turn of the Century*, (Kalliopi Koufa, editor), Thesaurus Acroasium, vol. 27, (1998), p. 69, espec. at pp. 92-97.

2. "New International Law and International Law-Making. New Thinking on Recognition and State Succession",in *Chinese Yearbook of International Law and Affairs*, (Chih-Yu Wu, Executive editor), vol. 16 (1997-1998)

3. "The International Lawyer as Jurisconsult in an Era of Historical Transition",in *Proceedings of the American Branch of the International Law Association*, 1997-1998 (John E. Noyes and Joel P. Trachtman, Editors), (1998), p. 57.

4. "International Law and the current conflict in Bosnia-Herzegovina",*Congress of the United States, Committee on Foreign Affairs, House of Representatives, Congressional Record*, E. 2542-3, August 12, 1992.

5. "The International Law of State Succession as applied to Yugoslavia, with particular reference to Bosnia and Herzegovina",*Congress of the United States, Committee on Foreign Affairs, House of Representatives, Congressional Record, Proceedings and Debates of the 103d. Congress, First Session*, vol. 139, no. 111, August 3, 1993.

6. "Self-determination of Peoples in Contemporary Constitutional and International Law",in *Liber Amicorum Judge Mohammed Bedjaoui*, (Emile Yakpo and Taha Boumedra, editors), (1999), p.725.

7. "Shifting paradigms of International Law and World Order in an era of historical transition",in *International Law in the Post-Cold War World*, (Wang Tieya and Sienho Yee, editors), (1999), p.1.

NOTES TO CHAPTER II

1. Thomas Kuhn, *The Structure of Scientific Revolutions* (1962).

2. Hans Kelsen, *Reine Rechtslehre* (1934); "The Pure Theory of Law", *Law Quarterly Review*, vol. 50, (1934), p. 474.

3. *International Law. A Textbook for Use in Law Schools* (F.I. Kozhevnikov, Editor), (1957), p. 16. The intellectual father and principal spokesman of the legal doctrine of Peaceful Coexistence was, however, Gregory Tunkin. See his Hague Academy lectures, "Coexistence and International Law", *Hague Recueil*, vol. 95 (1958) 1; and his article, "Sorok let sosyshchestvovania i mezhdunarodnoe pravo", *Sovetskii Ezhegodnik Mezdunarodnogo Prava*, vol. 1958 (1959), p. 15. A remarkable latter-day tribute to Tunkin's *rôle* in promoting East-West *détente* is contained in the symposium volume of essays by Western and Russian specialists, *From Coexistence to Cooperation. International Law and Organisation in the Post-Cold War Era.* (E. McWhinney, D. Ross, G. Tunkin, and V. Vereshchetin, Editors) (1991).

4. The highly developed special International Law-making processes of the Cold War era and their ultimate refinement and concretisation in the East-West Détente process are discussed in my earlier monographs, *"Peaceful Coexistence" and Soviet-Western International Law* (1964); *Conflict idéologique et Ordre public mondial* (1970); *The International Law of Détente. Arms Control, European Security and East-West Cooperation* (1978).

5. *The International Law of Détente* (1978), p. 39 et seq.; p. 70 et seq.; p. 167 et seq. And see also Nagendra Singh and E. McWhinney, *Nuclear Weapons and Contemporary International Law* (2nd rev. ed., 1989).

6. Samuel Huntington, *The Clash of Civilisations and the Remaking of the World Order* (1996).

7. Francis Fukuyama, *The End of History? The National Interest*, (1989), p. 3.

NOTES TO CHAPTER III

1. *Questions of Interpretation and Application of the 1971 Montreal Convention arising from the Aerial Incident at Lockerbie, Provisional Measures, (Libya v. U.K.),* I.C.J. Reports 1992, p. 3; *(Libya v. U.S.),* I.C.J. Reports 1992, p. 114. And see especially the Separate Opinion of Judge Lachs, *ibid.,* pp. 26-7, discussed in *Judge Manfred Lachs and Judicial Law Making. Opinions on the International Court of Justice, 1967-1993* (1995) at pp. 72-4, 82, 87.
2. See Boutros Boutros-Ghali, *Unvanquished, A U.S.-U.N. Saga* (1999), p. 265 et seq.

NOTES TO CHAPTER IV

1. The committee of the Norwegian Parliament which chooses the Nobel Peace Prize laureates each year, has, from its first award, in 1901, to International Red Cross founder, Henri Dunant, recognized non-governmental, non-profit, private, humanitarian organisations and groups. Other early awards were to the Institut de Droit International (1904) and to the Nansen Committee on Refugees. Most recently, the Nobel Peace Prize has gone to International Physicians for the Prevention of Nuclear War (1985); the Pugwash Movement for Nuclear Disarmament (1995); the International Campaign to Ban Landmines (1997); and the French organisation of private doctors, now active in 80 countries, Médecins Sans Frontières (1999). (See House of Commons (Canada), Debates, Official Report (Hansard), vol. 136, p. 261 (18 October 1999).

2. *R. v. Bow Street Metropolitan Stipendiary Magistrate, ex parte Pinochet Ugarte,* House of Lords, [1998] 3 W.L.R. 1456; [1999] 2 W.L.R. 827.

3. An excellent technical résumé of the successive rulings by the British courts is given by the German scholar, Thilo Rensmann, "Internationale Verbrechen und Befreiung von staatlicher Gerichtsbarkeit" *Praxis des Internationalen Privat – und Verfahrensrechts,* vol. 99, no. 4, (1999), p.268 et seq.

NOTES TO CHAPTER V

1. Gustav Radbruch's identification of legal antinomies and their rôle in decision-making is developed in his *Lehrbuch der Rechtsphilosophie* (3rd ed., 1932). There are some parallelisms to the U.S. legal philosopher, Wesley Newcomb Hohfeld's fundamental legal conceptions – the jural correlatives and jural opposites, as described in Hohfeld's posthumously published work, *Fundamental Legal Conceptions as applied in Judicial Reasoning* (1923). There does not seem to have been any direct link between the two jurists. Radbruch's legal antinomies concept was set out as part of his general philosophy of legal relativism, but seems unaffected by Radbruch's immediate post-World War II questioning of the political limits of his own relativist legal theory. Radbruch, *Vorschule zur Rechtsphilosophie* (1947); "Gesetzliches Unrecht und Übergesetzliches Recht", *Süddeutsche Juristen-Zeitung*, vol. 1, (1946), p. 105.

2. *Certain Expenses of the United Nations. Advisory Opinion.* I.C.J. Reports 1962, p. 151.

3. per Winiarski J., (President), *ibid.*, p. 230. (Dissenting Opinion).

4. per Koretsky, J., *ibid.*, p. 268. (Dissenting Opinion).
See the collected works, Jurisprudence for a Free society. Studies in Law, Science and Policy (2 vols.), (1992), by Harold D. Lasswell and Myres S. McDougal; (reviewed in extenso by the present writer, American Journal of International Law, vol. 87 (1993), at p. 225 et seq.).

5. See the collected works, Jurisprudence for a Free Society. Studies in Law, Science and Policy (2 vols.), (1992), by Harold D. Lasswell and Myres S. McDougal; (reviewed in extenso by the present writer, *American Journal of International Law*, vol. 87 (1993), at p. 225 et seq.).

6. *United Nations, Report of Special Committee on the Charter of the U.N. and on the strengthening of the Rôle of the Organisation* (December, 1982).

7. J.L. Brierly, *The Law of Nations* (4th ed., 1949); (6th ed., (Sir Humphrey Waldock, Editor), (1963), at p. 403), citing Lauterpacht (then Professor, and later British judge on the International Court of Justice, in *British Yearbook of International Law*, (1946), p. 46.

8. *Military and Paramilitary Activities in and against Nicaragua (Nicaragua v. U.S.A.), Merits, Judgment*, I.C.J. Reports 1986, p.14.

9. *Legal Consequences for States of the Continued Presence of South Africa in Namibia (South West Africa) notwithstanding Security Council Resolution 276 (1970),*

Advisory Opinion, I.C.J. Reports 1971, p. 16.

10. See, for example, *Rights of Minorities in Upper Silesia (Minority Schools)*, P.C.I.J., Series A, No. 12 (1928); *Rights of Minorities in Upper Silesia (Minority Schools)*, P.C.I.J., Series C, No. 14 (II); *Access to German Minority Schools in Upper Silesia, Advisory Opinion*, P.C.I.J., Series A/B, No. 40 (1931), 4-32; *Access to German Minority Schools in Upper Silesia*, P.C.I.J., Series C. No. 53.

11. *Exchange of Greek and Turkish Populations, Advisory Opinion*, P.C.I.J., Series B, No.10 (1925).

12. Julius Stone, *Aggression and World Order* (1958), pp. 99-100; Stone, *Legal Controls of International Conflict* (1954), p. 244, p. 262, p. 274; Stone, *Quest for Survival. The Rôle of Law and Foreign Policy* (1961), p. 47. On U.S. theories advanced at the time of, or immediately after the Cuban missile crisis of 1962, see Covey Oliver, "International law and the Quarantine of Cuba: a hopeful prescription for legal writing," *American Journal of International Law*, vol. 57, (1963), p. 373; Abe Chayes, "Cuban Quarantine: implications for the future", *Proceedings of the American Society of International Law* (1963), p. 10.

13. See, in the earlier, jurisdictional testing before the International Court of Justice, prior to the consensual, out-of-Court settlement, *Case concerning the Aerial Incident of 3 July 1988 (Islamic Republic of Iran v. U.S.A.), Order of 13 December 1989*, I.C.J. Reports 1989, p. 132. The preliminary, jurisdictional ruling of the International Court was made unanimously with, however, Judge Oda (Japan) also filing a Declaration, and with Judges Schwebel (U.S.A.) and Shahabuddeen (Guyana) filing Separate Opinions which involve a certain joinder of issue on the procedural points involved. And see, generally, *Judicial Settlement of International Disputes. Jurisdiction, Justiciability, and Judicial Law-Making on the Contemporary International Court* (1991), pp. 46-50, 55.

14. See, for example, *The Four Steps at Athens toward World Peace through Law* (World Peace through Law Centre, Washington, D.C.) (1963).

15. *Customs Régime between Germany and Austria, Advisory Opinion*, P.C.I.J., Series A/B, No. 41 (1931); *Customs Régime between Germany and Austria*, P.C.I.J., Series C, No. 53.

16. See, for example, *Case concerning Legality of Use of Force (Yugoslavia v. U.S.A.) Request for Indication of Provisional Measures*, (decision of 2 June 1999), I.C.J. Reports 1999. In *Yugoslavia v. U.S.A.*, the actual Court vote to refuse Provisional Measures to Yugoslavia was made by a 12-to-3 majority, with the Chinese and Russian judges and also the *ad hoc* judge designated by Yugoslavia dissenting. Three judges appended Declarations to the Order of the Court and two other judges appended Separate Opinions, while the *ad hoc* Yugoslav judge filed a Dissenting Opinion.

17. See *Case concerning the Aerial Incident of 3 July 1988 (Islamic Republic of Iran v. U.S.A.)*, I.C.J. Reports 1989, p. 132 (*supra*).

NOTES TO CHAPTER VI

1. *Western Sahara. Advisory Opinion*, I.C.J. Reports 1975, p.12. Dr. Bedjaoui's arguments, as legal counsel in his pleadings before the Court, were specifically adopted and approved by Judge Ammoun in his Separate Opinion, ibid., pp. 86-7. And see also Bedjaoui, *Terra nullius, 'droits' historiques et auto-détermination* (1975).

2. "International Law and the current conflict in Bosnia-Herzegovina", *Congressional Record*, E 2542-3, August 12, 1992: "The International Law of State Succession as applied to Yugoslavia, with particular reference to Bosnia and Herzegovina", *Congressional Record, Proceedings and Debates of the 103d Congress, First Session*, vol.139, no.111, August 3, 1993.

3. See, in this regard, Niall Ferguson, *The Pity of War. Explaining World War I* (1998); John Keegan, *The First World War* (1998).

4. Boutros Boutros-Ghali, *Unvanquished. A U.S.-U.N. Saga* (1999), pp. 87-8, 91-2.

5. Boutros-Ghali, *op. cit.* pp. 38-53, 114 et seq.

6. Dean Acheson, *Proceedings of the American Society of International Law* (1963), pp. 13-14. And see, also, *Conflit idéologique et Ordre public mondial* (1970), p. 29 *et seq.; Conflict and Compromise. International law and World Order in a Revolutionary Age* (1981), pp. 28-9.

7. Abe Chayes, "Law and the Quarantine of Cuba", *Foreign Affairs*, vol. 41 (1963), p. 550. And see also Chayes, "A Common Lawyer looks at International Law", *Harvard Law Review*, vol. 78 (1965, p. 1396).

8. *Canada: House of Commons Debates*, vol. 135, no. 134, 36th Parliament, Wednesday, October 7, 1998: pp. 8921-8927; *House of Commons Debates*, vol. 135, no. 205A, 36th Parliament, Monday, April 12, 1999: pp. 13613-13617; *House of Commons Debates*, vol. 135, no. 216, Tuesday, April 27, 1999, pp. 14360-14372.

9. Since the cessation of the NATO aerial bombardments in June, 1999, reports have emerged in Western media that NATO officials and political leaders may have deliberately distorted or exaggerated allegations of war crimes in Kosovo in the run up to the armed intervention. The first public questioning appears to have been by the British journal, *The Spectator*, reprinted in the *National Post* (Toronto), 4 November 1999. Retired Major-General Lewis MacKenzie of Canada, who commanded the United Nations forces in Bosnia in 1992, voiced similar misgivings in the extensive media debate that followed. (*The Globe and Mail* (Toronto), 9 November 1999.)

10. *United Nations Security Council*: Resolution 1264 (1999), (adopted by the Security Council at its 4045th meeting on 15 September 1999).

DOCUMENTS

1. G 8 Foreign Ministers: Statement by the Chairman on the conclusion of the meeting of the G 8 Foreign Ministers on the Petersberg, 6 May 1999

1. The G 8 Foreign Ministers adopted the following general principles on the political solution to the Kosovo crisis:
   - Immediate and verifiable end of violence and repression in Kosovo;
   - Withdrawal from Kosovo of military, police and paramilitary forces;
   - Deployment in Kosovo of effective international civil and security presences, endorsed and adopted by the United Nations, capable of guaranteeing the achievement of the common objectives;
   - Establishment of an interim administration for Kosovo to be decided by the Security Council of the United Nations to ensure conditions for a peaceful and normal life for all inhabitants in Kosovo;
   - The safe and free return of all refugees and displaced persons and unimpeded access to Kosovo by humanitarian aid organisations;
   - A political process towards the establishment of an interim political framework agreement providing for a substantial self-government for Kosovo, taking full account of the Rambouillet accords and the principles of sovereignty and territorial integrity of the Federal Republic of Yugoslavia and the other countries of the region, and the demilitarization of the UCK;
   - Comprehensive approach to the economic development and stabilization of the crisis region.

2. In order to implement these principles the G 8 Foreign Ministers instructed their Political Directors to prepare elements of a United Nations Security Council resolution.

3. The Political Directors will draw up a roadmap on further concrete steps towards a political solution to the Kosovo crisis.

4. The G 8 presidency will inform the Chinese government on the results

of today's meeting.

5. Foreign Ministers will reconvene in due time to review the progress which has been achieved up to that point.

United Nations Security Council Resolution 1244 (1999) adopted by the Security Council at its 4011th meeting, on 10 June 1999

The Security Council,

Bearing in mind the purposes and principles of the Charter of the United Nations, and the primary responsibility of the Security Council for the maintenance of international peace and security,

Recalling its resolutions 1160 (1998) of 31 March 1998, 1199 (1998) of 23 September 1998, 1203 (1998) of 24 October 1998 and 1239 (1999) of 14 May 1999,

Regretting that there has not been full compliance with the requirements of these resolutions,

Determined to resolve the grave humanitarian situation in Kosovo, Federal Republic of Yugoslavia, and to provide for the safe and free return of all refugees and displaced persons to their homes,

Condemning all acts of violence against the Kosovo population as well as all terrorist acts by any party,

Recalling the statement made by the Secretary-General on 9 April 1999, expressing concern at the humanitarian tragedy taking place in Kosovo,

Reaffirming the right of all refugees and displaced persons to return to their homes in safety,

Recalling the jurisdiction and the mandate of the International Tribunal for the Former Yugoslavia,

Welcoming the general principles on a political solution to the Kosovo crisis adopted on 6 May 1999 (S/1999/516, annex 1 to this resolution) and welcoming also the acceptance by the Federal Republic of Yugoslavia of the principles set forth in points 1 to 9 of the paper presented in Belgrade on 2 June 1999 (S/1999/649, annex 2 to this resolution), and the Federal

Republic of Yugoslavia's agreement to that paper,

Reaffirming the commitment of all Member States to the sovereignty and territorial integrity of the Federal Republic of Yugoslavia and the other States of the region, as set out in the Helsinki Final Act and annex 2,

Reaffirming the call in previous resolutions for substantial autonomy and meaningful self-administration for Kosovo,

Determining that the situation in the region continues to constitute a threat to international peace and security,

Determined to ensure the safety and security of international personnel and the implementation by all concerned of their responsibilities under the present resolution, and *acting* for these purposes under Chapter VII of the Charter of the United Nations,

1. *Decides* that a political solution to the Kosovo crisis shall be based on the general principles in annex 1 and as further elaborated in the principles and other required elements in annex 2;

2. *Welcomes* the acceptance by the Federal Republic of Yugoslavia of the principles and other required elements referred to in paragraph 1 above, and *demands* the full cooperation of the Federal Republic of Yugoslavia in their rapid implementation;

3. *Demands* in particular that the Federal Republic of Yugoslavia put an immediate and verifiable end to violence and repression in Kosovo, and begin and complete verifiable phased withdrawal from Kosovo of all military, police and paramilitary forces according to a rapid timetable, with which the deployment of the international security presence in Kosovo will be synchronized;

4. *Confirms* that after the withdrawal an agreed number of Yugoslav and Serb military and police personnel will be permitted to return to Kosovo to perform the functions in accordance with annex 2;

5. *Decides* on the deployment in Kosovo, under United Nations auspices, of international civil and security presences, with appropriate equipment and personnel as required, and welcomes the agreement of the Federal

Republic of Yugoslavia to such presences;

6. *Requests* the Secretary-General to appoint, in consultation with the Security Council, a Special Representative to control the implementation of the international civil presence, and *further requests* the Secretary-General to instruct his Special Representative to coordinate closely with the international security presence to ensure that both presences operate towards the same goals and in a mutually supportive manner;

7. *Authorizes* Member States and relevant international organizations to establish the international security presence in Kosovo as set out in point 4 of annex 2 with all necessary means to fulfil its responsibilities under paragraph 9 below;

8. *Affirms* the need for the rapid early deployment of effective international civil and security presences to Kosovo, and *demands* that the parties cooperate fully in their deployment;

9. *Decides* that the responsibilities of the international security presence to be deployed and acting in Kosovo will include:

(a) Deterring renewed hostilities, maintaining and where necessary enforcing a ceasefire, and ensuring the withdrawal and preventing the return into Kosovo of Federal and Republic military, police and paramilitary forces, except as provided in point 6 of annex 2;

(b) Demilitarizing the Kosovo Liberation Army (KLA) and other armed Kosovo Albanian groups as required in paragraph 15 below;

(c) Establishing a secure environment in which refugees and displaced persons can return home in safety, the international civil presence can operate, a transitional administration can be established, and humanitarian aid can be delivered;

(d) Ensuring public safety and order until the international civil presence can take responsibility for this task;

(e) Supervising demining until the international civil presence can, as appropriate, take over responsibility for this task;

(f) Supporting, as appropriate, and coordinating closely with the work of the international civil presence;

(g) Conducting border monitoring duties as required;

(h) Ensuring the protection and freedom of movement of itself, the international civil presence, and other international organizations;

10. *Authorizes* the Secretary-General, with the assistance of relevant international organizations, to establish an international civil presence in Kosovo in order to provide an interim administration for Kosovo under which the people of Kosovo can enjoy substantial autonomy within the Federal Republic of Yugoslavia, and which will provide transitional administration while establishing and overseeing the development of provisional democratic self-governing institutions to ensure conditions for a peaceful and normal life for all inhabitants of Kosovo;

11. *Decides* that the main responsibilities of the international civil presence will include:

(a) Promoting the establishment, pending a final settlement, of substantial autonomy and self-government in Kosovo, taking full account of annex 2 and of the Rambouillet accords (S/1999/648);

(b) Performing basic civilian administrative functions where and as long as required;

(c) Organizing and overseeing the development of provisional institutions for democratic and autonomous self-government pending a political settlement, including the holding of elections;

(d) Transferring, as these institutions are established, its administrative responsibilities while overseeing and supporting the consolidation of Kosovo's local provisional institutions and other peace-building activities;

(e) Facilitating a political process designed to determine Kosovo's future status, taking into account the Rambouillet accords (S/1999/648);

(f) In a final stage, overseeing the transfer of authority from Kosovo's provisional institutions to institutions established under a political settlement;

(g) Supporting the reconstruction of key infrastructure and other economic reconstruction;

(h) Supporting, in coordination with international humanitarian organizations, humanitarian and disaster relief aid;

(i) Maintaining civil law and order, including establishing local police forces and meanwhile through the deployment of international police personnel to serve in Kosovo;

(j) Protecting and promoting human rights;

(k) Assuring the safe and unimpeded return of all refugees and displaced persons to their homes in Kosovo;

12. *Emphasizes* the need for coordinated humanitarian relief operations, and for the Federal Republic of Yugoslavia to allow unimpeded access to Kosovo by humanitarian aid organizations and to cooperate with such organizations so as to ensure the fast and effective delivery of international aid;

13. *Encourages* all Member States and international organizations to contribute to economic and social reconstruction as well as to the safe return of refugees and displaced persons, and *emphasizes* in this context the importance of convening an international donors' conference, particularly for the purposes set out in paragraph 11 (g) above, at the earliest possible date;

14. *Demands* full cooperation by all concerned, including the international security presence, with the International Tribunal for the Former Yugoslavia;

15. *Demands* that the KLA and other armed Kosovo Albanian groups end immediately all offensive actions and comply with the requirements for demilitarization as laid down by the head of the international security presence in consultation with the Special Representative of the Secretary-General;

16. *Decides* that the prohibitions imposed by paragraph 8 of resolution 1160 (1998) shall not apply to arms and related *matériel* for the use of the international civil and security presences;

17. *Welcomes* the work in hand in the European Union and other international organizations to develop a comprehensive approach to the economic development and stabilization of the region affected by the Kosovo crisis, including the implementation of a Stability Pact for South Eastern Europe with broad international participation in order to further the promotion of democracy, economic prosperity, stability and regional cooperation;

18. *Demands* that all States in the region cooperate fully in the implementation of all aspects of this resolution;

19. *Decides* that the international civil and security presences are established for an initial period of 12 months, to continue thereafter unless the Security Council decides otherwise;

20. *Requests* the Secretary-General to report to the Council at regular intervals on the implementation of this resolution, including reports from the leaderships of the international civil and security presences, the first reports to be submitted within 30 days of the adoption of this resolution;

21. *Decides* to remain actively seized of the matter.

Annex 1

Statement by the Chairman on the conclusion of the meeting of the G-8 Foreign Ministers held at the Petersberg Centre on 6 May 1999

The G-8 Foreign Ministers adopted the following general principles on the political solution to the Kosovo crisis:

— Immediate and verifiable end of violence and repression in Kosovo;

— Withdrawal from Kosovo of military, police and paramilitary forces;

— Deployment in Kosovo of effective international civil and security presences, endorsed and adopted by the United Nations, capable of guaranteeing the achievement of the common objectives;

- Establishment of an interim administration for Kosovo to be decided by the Security Council of the United Nations to ensure conditions for a peaceful and normal life for all inhabitants in Kosovo;

- The safe and free return of all refugees and displaced persons and unimpeded access to Kosovo by humanitarian aid organizations;

- A political process towards the establishment of an interim political framework agreement providing for a substantial self-government for Kosovo, taking full account of the Rambouillet accords and the principles of sovereignty and territorial integrity of the Federal Republic of Yugoslavia and the other countries of the region, and the demilitarization of the KLA;

- Comprehensive approach to the economic development and stabilization of the crisis region.

Annex 2

Agreement should be reached on the following principles to move towards a resolution of the Kosovo crisis:

1. An immediate and verifiable end of violence and repression in Kosovo.

2. Verifiable withdrawal from Kosovo of all military, police and paramilitary forces according to a rapid timetable.

3. Deployment in Kosovo under United Nations auspices of effective international civil and security presences, acting as may be decided under Chapter VII of the Charter, capable of guaranteeing the achievement of common objectives.

4. The international security presence with substantial North Atlantic Treaty Organization participation must be deployed under unified command and control and authorized to establish a safe environment for all people in Kosovo and to facilitate the safe return to their homes of all dis-

placed persons and refugees.

5. Establishment of an interim administration for Kosovo as a part of the international civil presence under which the people of Kosovo can enjoy substantial autonomy within the Federal Republic of Yugoslavia, to be decided by the Security Council of the United Nations. The interim administration to provide transitional administration while establishing and overseeing the development of provisional democratic self-governing institutions to ensure conditions for a peaceful and normal life for all inhabitants in Kosovo.

6. After withdrawal, an agreed number of Yugoslav and Serbian personnel will be permitted to return to perform the following functions:

- Liaison with the international civil mission and the international security presence;

- Marking/clearing minefields;

- Maintaining a presence at Serb patrimonial sites;

- Maintaining a presence at key border crossings.

7. Safe and free return of all refugees and displaced persons under the supervision of the Office of the United Nations High Commissioner for Refugees and unimpeded access to Kosovo by humanitarian aid organizations.

8. A political process towards the establishment of an interim political framework agreement providing for substantial self-government for Kosovo, taking full account of the Rambouillet accords and the principles of sovereignty and territorial integrity of the Federal Republic of Yugoslavia and the other countries of the region, and the demilitarization of UCK. Negotiations between the parties for a settlement should not delay or disrupt the establishment of democratic self-governing institutions.

9. A comprehensive approach to the economic development and stabilization of the crisis region.
This will include the implementation of a stability pact for South-Eastern Europe with broad international participation in order to further promotion

of democracy, economic prosperity, stability and regional cooperation.

10. Suspension of military activity will require acceptance of the principles set forth above in addition to agreement to other, previously identified, required elements, which are specified in the footnote below.[1] A military-technical agreement will then be rapidly concluded that would, among other things, specify additional modalities, including the roles and functions of Yugoslav/Serb personnel in Kosovo:

Withdrawal

– Procedures for withdrawals, including the phased, detailed schedule and delineation of a buffer area in Serbia beyond which forces will be withdrawn;

Returning personnel

– Equipment associated with returning personnel;

– Terms of reference for their functional responsibilities;

– Timetable for their return;

– Delineation of their geographical areas of operation;

– Rules governing their relationship to the international security presence and the international civil mission.

Notes

1
Other required elements:

– A rapid and precise timetable for withdrawals, meaning, e.g., seven days to complete withdrawal and air defence weapons withdrawn outside a 25 kilometre mutual safety zone within 48 hours;

– Return of personnel for the four functions specified above will be under the supervision of the international security presence and will be limited to a small agreed number (hundreds, not thousands);

- Suspension of military activity will occur after the beginning of verifiable withdrawals;

- The discussion and achievement of a military-technical agreement shall not extend the previously determined time for completion of withdrawals.

3. Document: S/RES/1264 (1999)
   Date: 15 September 1999

United Nations Security Council Resolution 1264 (1999) adopted by the Security Council at its 4045th meeting, on 15 September 1999

The Security Council,

Recalling its previous resolutions and the statements of its President on the situation in East Timor,

Recalling also the Agreement between Indonesia and Portugal on the question of East Timor of 5 May 1999 and the Agreements between the United Nations and the Governments of Indonesia and Portugal of the same date regarding the modalities for the popular consultation of the East Timorese through a direct ballot and security arrangements (S/1999/513, Annexes I to III),

Reiterating its welcome for the successful conduct of the popular consultation of the East Timorese people of 30 August 1999 and *taking note* of its outcome, which it regards as an accurate reflection of the views of the East Timorese people,

Deeply concerned by the deterioration in the security situation in East Timor, and in particular by the continuing violence against and large-scale displacement and relocation of East Timorese civilians,

Deeply concerned also at the attacks on the staff and premises of the United Nations Mission in East Timor (UNAMET), on other officials and on international and national humanitarian personnel,

Recalling the relevant principles contained in the Convention on the Safety of United Nations and Associated Personnel adopted on 9 December 1994,

Appalled by the worsening humanitarian situation in East Timor, particularly as it affects women, children and other vulnerable groups,

Reaffirming the right of refugees and displaced persons to return in safety and security to their homes,

97

Endorsing the report of the Security Council Mission to Jakarta and Dili (S/1999/976),

Welcoming the statement by the President of Indonesia on 12 September 1999 in which he expressed the readiness of Indonesia to accept an international peacekeeping force through the United Nations in East Timor,

Welcoming the letter from the Minister for Foreign Affairs of Australia to the Secretary-General of 14 September 1999 (S/1999/975),

Reaffirming respect for the sovereignty and territorial integrity of Indonesia,

Expressing its concern at reports indicating that systematic, widespread and flagrant violations of international humanitarian and human rights law have been committed in East Timor, and *stressing* that persons committing such violations bear individual responsibility,

Determining that the present situation in East Timor constitutes a threat to peace and security,

Acting under Chapter VII of the Charter of the United Nations,

1. *Condemns* all acts of violence in East Timor, calls for their immediate end and demands that those responsible for such acts be brought to justice;

2. *Emphasizes* the urgent need for coordinated humanitarian assistance and the importance of allowing full, safe and unimpeded access by humanitarian organizations and *calls upon* all parties to cooperate with such organizations so as to ensure the protection of civilians at risk, the safe return of refugees and displaced persons and the effective delivery of humanitarian aid;

3. *Authorizes* the establishment of a multinational force under a unified command structure, pursuant to the request of the Government of Indonesia conveyed to the Secretary-General on 12 September 1999, with the following tasks: to restore peace and security in East Timor, to protect and support UNAMET in carrying out its tasks and, within force capabilities, to facilitate humanitarian assistance operations, and *authorizes* the States participating in the multinational force to take all necessary mea-

sures to fulfil this mandate;

4. *Welcomes* the expressed commitment of the Government of Indonesia to cooperate with the multinational force in all aspects of the implementation of its mandate and *looks forward* to close coordination between the multinational force and the Government of Indonesia;

5. *Underlines* the Government of Indonesia's continuing responsibility under the Agreements of 5 May 1999, taking into account the mandate of the multinational force set out in paragraph 3 above, to maintain peace and security in East Timor in the interim phase between the conclusion of the popular consultation and the start of the implementation of its result and to guarantee the security of the personnel and premises of UNAMET;

6. *Welcomes* the offers by Member States to organize, lead and contribute to the multinational force in East Timor, *calls on* Member States to make further contributions of personnel, equipment and other resources and *invites* Member States in a position to contribute to inform the leadership of the multinational force and the Secretary-General;

7. *Stresses* that it is the responsibility of the Indonesian authorities to take immediate and effective measures to ensure the safe return of refugees to East Timor;

8. *Notes* that Article 6 of the Agreement of 5 May 1999 states that the Governments of Indonesia and Portugal and the Secretary-General shall agree on arrangements for a peaceful and orderly transfer of authority in East Timor to the United Nations, and *requests* the leadership of the multinational force to cooperate closely with the United Nations to assist and support those arrangements;

9. *Stresses* that the expenses for the force will be borne by the participating Member States concerned and *requests* the Secretary-General to establish a trust fund through which contributions could be channelled to the States or operations concerned;

10. *Agrees* that the multinational force should collectively be deployed in East Timor until replaced as soon as possible by a United Nations peacekeeping operation, and *invites* the Secretary-General to make prompt recommendations on a peacekeeping operation to the Security Council;

11. *Invites* the Secretary-General to plan and prepare for a United Nations transitional administration in East Timor, incorporating a United Nations peacekeeping operation, to be deployed in the implementation phase of the popular consultation (phase III) and to make recommendations as soon as possible to the Security Council;

12. *Requests* the leadership of the multinational force to provide periodic reports on progress towards the implementation of its mandate through the Secretary-General to the Council, the first such report to be made within 14 days of the adoption of this resolution;

13. *Decides* to remain actively seized of the matter.

EDWARD MCWHINNEY,
Q.C., LL.M., S.J.D., LL.D., M.P.

Edward Watson McWhinney is Member of Parliament for Vancouver-Quadra. He has been, successively, Parliamentary Secretary (Fisheries) and Parliamentary Secretary (Foreign Affairs) in the Government of Canada.

Dr. McWhinney is a double graduate of Yale University, where he took his doctorate (in Constitutional and International Law). He went on to post-doctoral research work in The Hague, Berlin, Pisa, and Geneva.

He was a Lecturer and Assistant Professor at Yale University (in Law and Political Science) for four years, and afterwards held full Chairs at the University of Toronto Law School, McGill University (where he was also Director of the Air-Space Institute), Indiana University (where he was Director of International and Comparative Law), and most recently, Simon Fraser University in Vancouver. He was named (by special decree of the French Cabinet) Professeur-associé at the University of Paris I (Sorbonne) in 1968, and again in 1982, and 1985. He has been a Visiting Professor teaching at the University of Heidelberg and the Max-Planck-Institut in 1960-61 and 1990, the Meiji University in Tokyo, and The Hague Academy of International Law in 1973 and 1990. He has given special courses of lectures at the *Collège de France*, the University of Madrid, the National Autonomous University of Mexico, and other World centres. He was also a Member and Special Adviser of the Canadian delegation to the United Nations General Assembly for three years in the early 1980's.

In his professional life, he has been a Crown Prosecutor, Royal Commissioner of Enquiry, Consultant to the Secretary-General of the United Nations, Constitutional and International Law Adviser to several Quebec Premiers, the Premier of Ontario, the federal Government and a number of foreign Governments. He was a Member of the Permanent Court of Arbitration, The Hague (1985-1991).

Dr. McWhinney is the author of 25 books (two in French and one in German), and of 13 co-authored books, as well as some 500 scientific articles published or translated in nine different languages.

He is a Membre-Associé of the Académié Internationale de Droit Comparé.

Dr. McWhinney was elected to the Institut de Droit International (Geneva), in 1967, the first member elected from Canada to the century and a quarter-old academy. He has been elected President of the Institut for the two-year term 1999-2001.

By the same author:

1. Judicial Review in the English-speaking World (1st ed., 1956; 4th ed., 1969).
2. Föderalismus und Bundesverfassungsrecht, (1962).
3. Constitutionalism in Germany and the Federal Constitutional Court, (1962).
4. Comparative Federalism. States' Rights and National Power, (1st ed., 1962; 2nd ed., 1965).
5. "Peaceful Coexistence" and Soviet-Western International Law, (1964).
6. Federal Constitution-Making for a Multi-National World, (1966).
7. International Law and World Revolution, (1967).
8. Conflit idéologique et Ordre public mondial, (1970).
9. Parliamentary Privilege and the Publication of Parliamentary Debates, (1974).
10. The Illegal Diversion of Aircraft and International Law, (1975).
11. The International Law of Détente. Arms Control, European Security, and East-West Cooperation, (1978).
12. The World Court and the Contemporary International Law-Making Process, (1979).
13. Quebec and the Constitution. 1960-1978, (1979).
14. Conflict and Compromise. International Law and World Order in a Revolutionary Age, (1981).
15. Constitution-Making. Principles, Process, Practice, (1981).
16. Canada and the Constitution. 1979-1982. Patriation and the Charter of Rights, (1982).
17. (a) United Nations Law-Making. Cultural and Ideological Relativism and International Law Making for an Era of Transition, (1984).
    (b) (French Language Edition): Les Nations Unies et la Formation du Droit, (1986).
18. Supreme Courts and Judicial Law-Making. Constitutional Tribunals and Constitutional Review, (1986).
19. Aerial Piracy and International Terrorism, (1987).
20. The International Court of Justice and the Western Tradition of International Law (the Paul Martin Lectures), (1987).
21. Nuclear Weapons and Contemporary International Law, (1989) (with President Nagendra Singh).
22. Judicial Settlement of International Disputes. Jurisdiction,

Justiciability and Judicial Law-Making on the Contemporary International Court (1991).

23. Judge Shigeru Oda and the Progressive Development of International Law: Opinions on the International Court of Justice, 1976-1992, (1993).

24. Judge Manfred Lachs and Judicial Law-Making: Opinions on the International Court of Justice, 1967-1993, (1995).

INDEX

Nuclear Weapons club 23-4
Nuremberg Tribunal 45

One World 4
Ottoman Empire 57-61
Owen-Stoltenberg Plan
 (Bosnia-Herzegovina) 20

Pakistan 23
Palmerston, Lord 32
Paradigm shift 4-6,50
Participatory democracy 21-2
Pax americana 13
Pax britannica 13
Pax sovietica-americana 6
Peaceful Coexistence xi-xii,
 6-10, 43, 79
People's Power 21-2
Petersberg statement (G-8)
 71-2, 86-7
Pinochet, General (Chile)
 24-5, 56-81
Plebiscites (League of Nations)
 35-6
Population transfers 35-6, 82
Post-Cold War era 13-16
Potsdam conference, 1945
 11, 36, 67
Prosecutor, ad hoc War Crimes
 tribunal 54-5, 75
Protocols, Additional (Aerial
 bombardment) 46-50, 75

Radbruch, Gustav 26, 82
Radojkovic, Milos xi, 7
Rambouillet Accord 68
Recognition of States 62-5
Realpolitik 10
Regional associations, U.N. 43-4
Reprisals 31-2

Robinson, Mary, 22
Roosevelt, Eleanor 4
Roosevelt, President Franklin
 (U.S.) 5
Rule of Law, World 50-1, 83
Rules of the Game, Cold War
 10-12
Rusk, Dean 72
Russia 58

San Stefano, Treaty, 1878 58
Schwarzenberger, G. 33
Secretary-General, U.N. 30-1
Security Council, U.N. 14, 30-1
Self-defence, principle 14, 42-3
Self-determination 9, 34-8
Serbia 60-1
Serbs, Croats, and Slovenes,
 Kingdom xi-xii,61-65
Simitis, Prime Minister (Greece)
 71
Slovenia 64
Sohn, Louis 50
Soviet bloc 26-7
Soviet Union 26-7
Spheres of Influence 11
Stalin, J. xi, 6, 70
St. Germain-en-Laye, Treaty 35
Stone, Julius 42, 83
Succession, State 20
Summit Meetings 5

Temperamenta belli 46-50
Territorial integrity 34-8
Tito, Marshal, 1, 20, 57, 61, 70
Transition, era 1-2
Truman, President Harry (U.S.)
 4, 15-16, 28-9, 67
Tunkin, Gregory 5-6, 79
Turkey 32